EXPLANATION
AND MEANING

EXPLANATION AND MEANING

AN INTRODUCTION TO PHILOSOPHY

DANIEL M. TAYLOR

Lecturer in Philosophy at the
University of Kent

CAMBRIDGE
AT THE UNIVERSITY PRESS
1970

Published by the Syndics of the Cambridge University Press
Bentley House, 200 Euston Road, London NW1 2DB
American Branch: 32 East 57th Street, New York, N.Y.10022

© Cambridge University Press 1970

Library of Congress Catalogue Card Number: 73-116837

ISBNS
0 521 07910 1 hard covers
0 521 09617 0 paperback

First published 1970
Reprinted 1973

First printed in Great Britain by
Alden & Mowbray Ltd
at the Alden Press, Oxford
Reprinted in Malta by
St Paul's Press Ltd

CONTENTS

v

ACKNOWLEDGEMENTS

I am grateful to Dr Peter Stone, Professor Patrick Nowell-Smith and Professor Bernard Williams for their criticisms of drafts of this book.

PREFACE

THIS book is intended as an introduction to philosophy. As such it might be expected to contain chapters dealing in turn with problems from each of the main areas of philosophy, epistemology, metaphysics, ethics, aesthetics, and logic. A great variety of these problems are in fact mentioned and discussed. Nevertheless the organisation of the book around two topics, meaning and explanation, requires justification.

The concepts of explanation and meaning are peculiarly important in philosophy. They are fundamentally involved in theories and problems belonging to every branch of the subject. It is difficult to define philosophy but three very general types of question together seem to express the purpose of most philosophical enquiries.

What is x? What is truth, beauty, knowledge, goodness, God, man etc.?

How is x to be explained? How can we explain the action of mind on matter, the sequence of events in the physical world, the origin of the world, the existence of evil?

What justifies us in believing x? Why should we believe that there is an external world, that events will continue in the future as in the past, that there is a God, that this thing is good or that action right?

When a philosopher asks "What is knowledge, or truth?" he does not seek a list of truths or an encyclopaedia of knowledge. His purpose is to understand the concepts of knowledge and truth, to be able to explain what it *means* to say that something is known as distinct from e.g. its being believed, or that a proposition is true as distinct from e.g.

its being probable or generally accepted. His question is then about meaning and to answer it he must have a view as to how meaning is to be determined, i.e. a theory of meaning.

The second type of question is clearly directly concerned with explanation, and the third also, for to justify a belief is to explain why one holds it.

Since questions about meaning and explanation are fundamental in any philosophical enquiry, the discussion of these concepts provides a convenient way of introducing a great variety of traditional philosophical problems. Among the problems considered here are those concerning causation, induction, scientific laws, reason and rationality, the justification of moral and aesthetic judgements, the explanation of human behaviour, behaviourist theories of mind, knowledge and understanding, sense and reference, universals, synonymy, interpretation, definition and inference. Each chapter raises one or other of these issues and a reading list is provided to assist further study.

Modern philosophers tend to be critical of metaphysical theories. Their own views, by contrast, sometimes appear unsystematic, their treatment of traditional problems piecemeal. It is often not apparent to someone beginning philosophy that their arguments on particular issues have any generality, or that there is any way of relating them to form a general theory. This impression may be difficult to correct in an introduction aimed simply at presenting a range of traditional philosophical problems. On the other hand, by concentrating on explanation and meaning it is possible to set out some of the very general arguments and distinctions which a modern philosopher might bring to a particular problem and at the same time to show how they may be brought together to form theories with a wide application.

Philosophers' interest in problems of meaning, truth, knowledge, explanation etc., has rarely been simply academic. In the past their aim has been, by examining these concepts, to establish conclusions of morality, religion or science. Thus, for example, Berkeley sought to prove God's existence from an examination of the nature of human knowledge. An important aim of this book is to show a beginner how philosophical theories and arguments have implications not just in the realms of religion and morality but also for his day to day discussions about historical events, literature or human behaviour. Philosophy should be more than just an academic discipline; it should be of use to those whose *main* interest lies in other areas. It seemed that the best hope of achieving this was by an introduction based on a systematic treatment of explanation and meaning. The implications of philosophical theories for other subjects are illustrated by examples from fields familiar to most people, literary criticism, history and social science.

This book originated in an introductory course in philosophy designed for students of history, literature and science as well as for those doing philosophy. It might serve as a text for interdisciplinary courses elsewhere.

D.M.T.

CHAPTER I

EXPLANATION: INTRODUCTION

WHAT is an explanation? There are a variety of theories about what it is really to explain, about what a proper explanation ought to be like. It might seem, then, that our problem is to choose between them. Some people argue, for example, that no explanation is worthy of the name unless it tells us the purpose of things, others that a complete and adequate explanation of everything can be given in terms of the laws of nature which govern the behaviour of matter. Some, again, claim that to explain is really just to describe, others that genuine explanation involves going beyond description. The aim of explanation is held by some to be understanding and by others to be the ability to predict and control events. These differences of opinion reflect disputes about what explanation 'really' is, or about what a 'real' explanation is.

Disputes of this kind are in a sense fruitless. Problems about whether something is a real x or not are often to be dissolved by noticing what the word "real" means in that particular context. One is clear about the difference between real butter and margarine, real silk and artificial silk, a real zebra and a mottled horse. The contrasts are between natural animal and vegetable fats, natural and man-made fibres, and between animals with differing physiological characteristics. But now suppose that butter is manufactured artificially as 'arfut', which has the same chemical structure as butter but does not come from a cow. Or suppose that it is discovered that some seeming zebras are more spotty than stripey. There might be lengthy arguments about whether arfut is really butter, or a spotty zebra a real zebra. The facts, however, are simple. Butter and arfut are to all appearances the same but they have different origins; the stripey and spotty zebras are identical except for one aspect of their appearance.

The word "real" is used to mark off things that are in many respects like other things but in important ways different. The crucial word here is "important". It is important to consumers and dairymen to distinguish butter from margarine. It is less important to consumers but still important to dairymen to distinguish butter from arfut. It might be important to distinguish spotty zebras from stripey zebras because of a significant difference in the genetic history of the animals, or it might be that there was a zebra fanciers' society with strict rules about acceptable markings.

The problem, then, with explanation will not be to argue whether scientific, or teleological, or narrative, or everyday explanations are real explanations. It will be to discover the facts about differences between various sorts of explanation, if there *are* differences, and then to determine how important these differences are in terms of the consequences flowing from them.

One way of approaching the subject is to examine as many examples of explanation as possible from various fields. Such a procedure would, however, prove very complex. The course adopted here is rather to begin by distinguishing three main kinds of explanation, then to show how this system of classification may be applied to explanations in various fields.

The classification of types of explanation adopted is the following.

Scientific Explanation. A scientific explanation must be such as to show why something had to happen. To give one involves hypothesising a law of nature and the explanation will only be correct if the hypothesis is true. Since the hypothesised law of nature may always turn out, upon further investigation, to be false, any explanation of this type is always open to later correction.

What-explanations. A what-explanation simply makes clear what something or some sequence of events is. One can distinguish between explanations of this type which relate events and objects to scientific theories and those which have little theoretical interest but which are intimately connected with decisions about action.

Reason-giving Explanation. Very often when we explain why we believe this or do that we are not hypothesising about the causes of our beliefs or actions. Instead we are attempting to influence the assessments or evaluations which others make of us, or of our beliefs and actions. We do this by explaining why we thought the action or belief satisfactory or correct.

Teleological explanations and explanations in terms of purposes are not treated separately. They do not form a homogeneous class. Some of them seem to be scientific, namely those which explain the behaviour of control mechanisms. Others may be what-explanations in terms of mental concepts, e.g. when we explain a man's behaviour by hypothesising about his purposes, aims or goals. Others still are reason-giving explanations as when we explain an action of our own by giving, as our reason for doing it, the purpose we wished to achieve.

The problem of what it is to explain the meaning of something is dealt with in the second half of this book.

CHAPTER 2

SCIENTIFIC EXPLANATION

THERE is one view of explanation which is especially clear and elegant. This view, associated with the name of an American philosopher, Hempel, is called the covering law model of explanation. Its advocates often put it forward as a definition of what any explanation must be like if it is to be satisfactory. Whether or not this is so, it does seem to be a correct account of what explanation is, and ought to be, in one major field, that of science.

We look to the sciences for explanations which tell us why things are as they are, that is, how they came to be as they are now. Such explanations inform us about the way one state of the world, or of a part of it, changes to another state; they involve principles of change. The chief questions to which these explanations provide an answer are: Why did this happen? Why have things changed, or developed in this way rather than that? Why, when this happens, does that happen?

Initially, one thinks of such questions as requests for causes: What caused this event? What caused things to develop in this way rather than that? And causes seem to most of us to be events or states of affairs which bring about or produce certain other events or states of affairs which we call their effects. Thus we think of science as investigating the causes of earthquakes, physical disease, explosions, mental illness, chemical reactions, and so on.

This simple idea of a cause is that of an event or state which (1) is prior to the event whose occurrence it is supposed to explain, and (2) necessitates, or makes happen this event.

4

Drinking poison both precedes and produces a death. The impact of one billiard ball brings about the subsequent movement of another billiard ball. As information of this type accumulates one is able to give explanations of classes of events; smoking causes cancer, drunkeness causes accidents, drinking arsenic causes death, and so on. However two points must be noticed about these investigations into causes.

(1) The event or state which is picked out as the cause of another particular event, or of a class of such events, is always only one of a set of events or states which are all equally necessary to the occurrence of the event to be explained. For example, we may seek to explain a fire in a hayrick by saying that it was caused by a cigarette end. But without oxygen and without the combustibility of the hay in the rick, the fire would not have occurred. These elements of the situation were equally necessary for the occurrence of the fire. Yet, and here is the problem, although the presence of oxygen is obviously part of the cause of the fire, one could not say that the presence of oxygen *produced* the fire. What then is the relationship between them? It is that whenever there is a fire oxygen is present; the two things just go together.

(2) When we look at the matter closely the notion of one event necessitating another is senseless. In fact one is confronted by a dilemma. If a and b are events then either a is a different event from b, in which case it is possible for a to occur without b occurring and vice versa, or it is impossible for a to occur without b and vice versa, in which case a and b are not different events. In other words, if two events are necessarily connected so that the occurrence of one necessitates the occurrence of the other, then the events are the same. This is a difficult thesis to prove but it can be supported

by the following argument. Consider the case of events separated in time. Two events separated in time must be different events. Yet one cannot necessitate the other, for suppose that the first occurs at a time t_1: if the world came to an end then, as it might, the second would not occur. To take an example, suppose the event at t_1 to be drinking poison and the other event to be the death of the drinker; so long as there is a time gap between the two it is always possible to stop the occurrence of the second event, death, by, for example, preventing the liquid from getting to the stomach. In face of this argument it might be suggested that one should take as the first event both the drinking of poison and its passage through the stomach into the blood stream. But even then: antidotes may be used. The only way to establish a necessary connection between the events is by making the first event *include* the cessation of the heartbeat and breathing as the poison reaches the brain. But now of course the first event is no longer different from the second: it is itself death. Moreover, the two events are no longer separated in time.

Now consider the case where two events are contemporaneous. Two contemporaneous events can be the same event and if the occurrence of the one necessitates the occurrence of the other, they *must* be the same event. For what does the word "necessitate" mean? It means that if event a occurs, event b must occur and cannot possibly not occur. But the only cases in which this is true are cases of events which are related by definition, and where things are related by definition, they are in a sense the same thing. If X becomes a brother (event a), he must become a male sibling (event b). If X becomes a husband (event a), someone else must become a wife (event b). In each case becoming the one thing is becoming the other, and to maintain the opposite would be to contradict oneself. But this is never true for events which are not related by definition and which are really different. The breaking of the stem of an apple does not necessitate the apple's beginning to fall. The one could happen and the other not if, for example, the apple were supported in another way. Nor is it true that the breaking of the apple stem and the apple's being unsupported together necessitate the apple's beginning to fall, for the apple may be floating freely in space. On the other hand, if we say that the apple's stem breaking, the apple's being unsupported and the operation of gravity necessitate the apple beginning to fall, we no longer have two separate events because in these circumstances the operation of gravity is the same as the apple's beginning to fall.

Scientists do try to discover how events are connected and they do try to show how the occurrence of certain events is necessary given certain facts, but the way they do this is not by discovering causes which both precede and necessitate their effects. The clue to what the scientist does in explaining change appeared in our discussion of the burning hayrick. Oxygen was a necessary condition of the fire. It is always present when there is a fire. The scientist looks for general laws, or universal propositions of the form: Whenever an event of type a occurs, an event of type b occurs. These universal propositions express the connections between events which figure in scientific explanations. But these laws, or universal generalisations, do not express a necessary connection, they express a contingent, or factual, connection. Examples of such propositions are the following: whenever a gas is heated, its volume remaining constant, its pressure rises; bodies attract one another with a force proportional to their mass and inversely proportional to the square of their distance. To give an explanation of why an event occurs is to show how it is related to other events by such universal generalisation.

THE COVERING LAW MODEL OF EXPLANATION

An explanation of an event a consists of three elements:

(1) a universal generalisation, or law statement: whenever an event of type b happens, an event of type a happens;

(2) a statement of initial conditions: b happened;

(3) a statement of the consequent conditions: a happened. For example:

(1) volume held constant, the pressure of a gas increases with increasing temperature;

(2) gas x in container y, which is of fixed volume, was heated between time $t1$ and $t2$;

(3) the pressure of gas x in container y increased between $t1$ and $t2$.

There are several features of this model to be noted. One may well call the event mentioned under (2) the cause of the event mentioned under (3) but notice that (2) by itself does not necessitate (3). However, if (1) is true and (2) is true, (3) must be true, so that the *truth* of (1) and (2) necessitates the *truth* of (3). Of course what necessiates (3) on this account is not an event but the truth of a general law and the truth of a statement of initial conditions. The necessity arises from the fact that the three propositions form a valid argument with (3) as the conclusion, and it is the definition of a valid argument that if the premises are true, then the conclusion *must* be true. The relationship between (1), (2) and (3) may also be expressed by saying that if the generalisation in (1) is true then, given the facts stated in (2), the event mentioned in (3) must occur. Sometimes we take the truth of physical laws for granted and simply say, for example, given the facts in (2) the event in (3) had to occur. But this is to speak elliptically.

The relation of (1) and (2) to (3), then, is the relation of premises to conclusion in a valid argument. This is one of the most interesting characteristics of this model of explanation for it treats the explanation of an event as the deduction, by valid argument, of the event's occurrence from some set of true premises. Consequently, what is true of valid deductive arguments will also be true of explanations of this type; we shall see the importance of this in the next chapter.

There is no essential difference on this model between the method of explaining particular events and that of explaining laws. As particular events are explained by deducing their occurrence from premises which include laws and statements of initial conditions, so laws are explained by deducing them from other laws, or from laws together with definitions. So that just as we are able to say that, given the truth of a universal generalisation and of certain statements of initial conditions, a particular event has to happen, so we are able to say that, given the truth of certain universal generalisations, other universal generalisations must be true. For example:

(1) as temperature rises the rate of movement of particles of a gas increases;

(2) as the rate of movement of particles of a gas increases the rate of incidence of the particles on the walls of the container increases;

(3) as the rate of incidence of particles on the container walls increases measured pressure goes up;

(4) as the temperature of a gas rises, pressure increases.

There are two features of the Hempelian model which are particularly interesting. The first is that the statements in the explanation logically entail the statement that the event being explained occurred. (This term "entail" is used by logicians to refer to the relation between propositions, or groups of propositions, which holds when the step from one to the other is a valid deductive inference. In any valid argument the premises taken together entail the conclusion. But entailment also holds between certain pairs of statements, for example, "John is a bachelor" entails "John is unmarried".)

The second is that the explanation must contain a universal generalisation. These two features are linked and if we accept the first we must accept the second.

Why should one accept the view that a scientific explanation must entail what it explains? Suppose that I wish to explain why Fred knifed Jake; I say that Fred hated Jake. But the statement, "Fred hated Jake" does not entail the statement, "Fred knifed Jake"; the one could be true and the other false. This means that it was possible for Fred to hate Jake and not knife him (he might have punched him, or ruined his career, or done nothing). The explanation given fails to tell us why *one* thing happened (the knifing) and not *another*. Hence it fails to tell us why Fred knifed Jake. Again, suppose that I wish to explain why Fred is delinquent; my explanation is that Fred comes from a broken home and many children from broken homes are delinquent:

(1) many children from broken homes are delinquent;
(2) Fred is from a broken home;
(3) Fred is a delinquent.

But this proffered explanation, (1) and (2), does not entail the thing to be explained, (3), for the propositions (1), (2) and (3) do not form a valid argument with (3) as the conclusion. Since some children from broken homes are not delinquent, (1) and (2) could be true and (3) false. Mentioning (1) and (2) fails to explain (3), for (1) and (2) do not tell us why Fred should be one of those from broken homes who are delinquent, rather than one of those from broken homes who are not. The situation would have been quite different if (1) had been "all children of broken homes are delinquent". Generally, if we wish to explain some happening stated in *h* by some set of statements *e where* e *does not entail* h, then the supposition that *e* is true leaves open the possibility both that *h* is true and that something else is true (that *h* is true, or that it is false). Where *e* does not entail *h* the supposition that *e* is true fails to tell us why *h* occurred and not something else, hence it fails to explain why *h* occurred.

Why must an explanation contain a universal generalisation? Unless explanations contain universal generalisations they will not entail what they are supposed to explain except in very special circumstances. The reader may test this for himself by trying to construct valid inferences from a statement asserting the occurrence of one state of affairs to a statement asserting' the occurrence of another without the use of a universal generalisation. He will find that it is possible only where the two states of affairs are in fact one, that is, where there is a definitional connection between them, hence no possibility of an explanation. To explain why, for example, Jones is a bachelor by saying that he is unmarried could only be a weak joke; a thing cannot explain its own occurrence.

It seems, then, that if scientific explanation consists in showing why something happened by showing that it had to happen because certain other things happened, then it must conform to the covering law model. Many explanations are however put forward in the form "*a* happened because *b* happened" without any mention of a universal generalisation (the apple fell because the stem was cut, he forgot her name because he wanted to forget her, he is delinquent because he is from a broken home.) The important consequence of the argument in this chapter is that if anyone puts forward an explanation of this kind claiming that it is scientific, or that it shows why *a* happened and not something else, he is implicitly asserting a universal generalisation. Unless there were such an implied assertion the mention of event *b* *could* not be sufficient to explain the occurrence of *a*. In fact one could say that the mention of an event *b* as showing why something *a* had to happen logically commits the speaker to accepting a universal generalisation connecting events of type *a* with events of type *b*.

It might be objected that we often do explain an event by saying, "*x* occurred because of *y*", e.g. the car crashed because it skidded, though we might deny that wherever *y* happens, *x* happens. Yet consider the following conversation:
– *A*: The accident occurred because the car skidded.
– *B*: Do you mean that whenever a car skids it crashes?
– *A*: No.
– *B*: Then you have not explained why this car crashed on this occasion.

But suppose that only one factor had changed prior to *x*; *y* happened. It might seem that in *this* case, whether or not events like *x* universally succeed events like *y*, *x* is explained by *y*. But if anything explains *x* in this imaginary example it is not *y* but y's *occurrence all else remaining constant* in some state *s*. Moreover even this will not explain *x* unless it is implied that events like *x* always occur in this combination of circumstances. A universal generalisation is still required.

Besides it can never be the case that all factors except one are constant. This would imply that nothing else changed anywhere in the world. To suppose instead that all but one of the *relevant* factors remained constant would imply a general theory as to the factors determining events such as *x*.

However it is only when someone claims to *explain* an event by saying "*x* occurred because of *y*" that he implies a universal generalisation relating *x*s and *y*s. There are other uses of the sentence which do not carry this implication.

A common use of the sentence, "*x* occurred because of *y*", is to assert that *x* would not have occurred but for *y*. Now a man may have died by the knife, yet it would be false to say that he would have lived but for being stabbed, if he had also been poisoned. Hence the assertion that *x* would not have occurred but for *y* must imply knowledge of what would have happened in the alternative situation; it must implicitly contrast what actually happened with what supposedly would have happened had *y* not occurred. Thus, e.g. if the car had not skidded (*y*), it would have continued normally (*z*) instead of crashing (*x*). Such an assertion is not an explanation of *x* but a comment about explanations of *x* and *z*. The claim is that, given the circumstances and the relevant laws, *x* is explicable and would have been predicted, but that if the circumstances had differed in one respect, *y* had not occurred, then *z* rather than *x* would have been predicted, and *z* alone would have been explicable.

Our interest in such a case is not so much in the explanation of x as in why x occurred rather than z, i.e. in the difference between the explanation of x and what would have been the explanation of z, had z occurred.

We sometimes say "x happened because of y" simply to announce a discovery, either of a particular fact about x, or a general fact concerning the relation between events such as x and y. In such cases, although an explanation is not given, it is implied that the discovery makes one possible. But it is not implied that y alone will provide it.

Finally, the purpose in claiming that x happened because of y may be a moral or a legal one. It may be to select one factor, among the many contributing to the occurrence of x, as solely, or mainly responsible for x. Now to attribute responsibility for x to y is not to explain x, it is e.g. to blame y. Nevertheless it must be implied that but for y, x would not have occurred. Consequently one is not justified in ascribing responsibility to something y unless one has good reason to believe this to be true, e.g. one knows the explanation of x.

STATISTICAL LAWS AND PROBABILISTIC EXPLANATIONS

Hempel recognises two types of scientific explanation, Deductive and Probabilistic, the former employing universal, the latter statistical generalisations. He gives the following as an example of probabilistic explanation:

(1) there is a high probability of a person who has been in contact with a case of measles catching measles;

(2) A has been in contact with a case of measles;

(3) A has measles (is highly probable).

Hempel argues that (1) and (2) give a high degree of credence to (3), not as high as would be the case if they entailed (3), but high enough to say that they explain it. But in fact (1) and (2) do not explain why A caught measles, for the question why A was one of those who catch measles after contact rather than one of those who do not remains unanswered. Moreover if we knew what determined in which of these classes a man fell, we should be able to assert a universal generalisation relating it and contact with measles to infection.

However, if a negative universal generalisation relating illness and contact were known, for example, that no one catches measles who has not been in contact with it, it would be possible to describe contact as a necessary condition of infection, hence necessarily *part* of the explanation of infection. It is perhaps our belief that this is so which inclines us to think of (1) and (2) above as to some extent explaining (3).

It might seem that statistical generalisations could be used if not to explain, then to predict particular events. For example if 90% of male smokers die of cancer and Fred smokes, it might appear that his death from cancer could be predicted with a probability of 0.9. Now either Fred will die of cancer or he will not, but the statement that the probability of his dying of cancer is 0.9 predicts neither of these outcomes. In fact probability statements about individuals should be interpreted as statements about the frequency of an event among a *set* of individuals. Thus the remark about Fred might mean "Nine out of ten male smokers, of which Fred is one, die of cancer", or "Predictions that a male smoker will die of cancer (of which this statement about Fred is one) are correct nine times out of ten".

Alternatively we might regard statistical generalisations as warranting, or supporting *categorical* predictions. One is certainly inclined to believe that Fred will die of cancer if 90% of smokers die of it. But it is one thing to be *inclined*, even with good reason, to predict an event, and quite another to be *able* to do so. Statistical generalisations only *enable* us to make inferences about the frequency of events of a particular kind. Moreover it is questionable whether even these inferences should be called predictions or explanations.

Consider the following inference *a*:

(1) 30% of *x*s are *y*s;

(2) $x_1 \ldots x_N$ are random samples of *n* drawn from the population of *x*s (where *n* is large);

(3) The mean percentage of *y*s in $x_1 \ldots x_N$ is 30%.

Now although (3) follows logically from (1) and (2), the fact reported in (3) is not explained by them.

Compare the following inference, *b*:

(1) all unsupported bodies fall;

(2) this apple was unsupported;

(3) this apple fell.

In *a* (1) and (2) entail (3), and the same is true of *b*. But in *a*, though not in *b*, it is also possible to deduce (1) from (2) and (3). It is this which precludes the use of inferences such as *a* to explain, or predict.

We can best appreciate this by supposing the propositions in *b* to be related in the same way as those in *a* and observing the consequences. If it were possible to deduce (1) in *b* from (2) and (3), then (2) and (3) would contain all that is asserted in (1) (for they would imply it). Thus in so far as *b* explained (3) the facts stated in (2) and (3) would provide the explanation. Now the fact that an apple fell (3) cannot explain itself, so it would be left to (2) alone to explain (3). But the fact that the apple was unsupported does not constitute, by itself, an explanation of the fact that it fell. Hence if *b* were in fact logically similar to *a* it would not provide any explanation of the event described by (3), nor could it be used to make predictions about similar events.

This is an indirect argument, but it suggests that statistical inference, although deductive, does not conform to the deductive model of explanation. In fact (2) in *a* is not an empirical statement about samples of *x*s. A sample is random only if each member of the population has the same chance of being picked for it, and this cannot be determined from an examination of a given sample. The result is that (3) simply represents a mathematical fact about the population described in (1).

CHAPTER 3

THE CONFIRMATION OF
SCIENTIFIC EXPLANATION

THE covering law model is a simple one. An event is to be explained by showing that, given the truth of a universal generalisation about the way the world and its parts work, and given the particular circumstances, then the event had to happen (its occurrence was deducible by logic). If one wants to explain why the universal generalisation holds, one does so by showing that if certain other universal generalisations (often more general than the one being explained) are true, then this one must be true. One may well ask at this point how one is to explain the most general universal generalisations, and this is a problem. Another difficulty arises from the fact that some generalisations seem to be unfit for explanation, for example the generalisation in the following 'explanation':

– Why are people getting out of bed in London?
– Because people are going to bed in New York.
– When people go to bed in New York people get up in London.

It is extremely difficult to say just what distinguishes the generalisations which are satisfactory in explanations from those which are not. We regard as explanatory generalisations which warrant the assertion of counterfactual propositions, i.e. propositions about what would have happened had circumstances been different. Non-explanatory or coincidental generalisations are those which appear to be true because of some special circumstances of time and place, e.g. all the coins in my pocket are copper. But why some generalisations are regarded in one way and some in the other remains unclear.

One can ask two types of question about a proffered explanation and they must be kept separate:

(1) *is* it an explanation? (2) is it *the correct* explanation? The covering law model supplies an answer to the first. It is that an explanation consists of a set of propositions from which it follows logically (in the way a conclusion follows from premises in a valid argument) that the event which is to be explained occurred. The model provides a way of deciding whether or not something *is* an explanation, but it leaves open the question whether or not it is the correct, or true, explanation. This is necessarily so. On the covering law model an explanation, with what it explains, forms a valid argument. But an argument, though valid, may yet contain only false propositions. For example:

(1) all dogs are fish;   (2) all cats are dogs;
                (3) therefore, all cats are fish.

To say that (1) and (2) in this example entail (3), or that (3) follows logically from (1) and (2) is not to imply that (1), (2), or (3) is true. To say that the argument is valid is simply to say that *if* (1) and (2) are true, then (3) *must* be true.

Moreover, several valid arguments with different premises may have the same conclusion. For example:

                all trees are fish;
                all cats are trees;
                therefore all cats are fish.

all fish are mammals;   all dogs are mammals;
all spaniels are fish;   all spaniels are dogs;
therefore all spaniels are   therefore all spaniels are
    mammals.   mammals.

all men with strong attachment to the father become homosexual; Jones has a strong attachment to his father; therefore Jones is homosexual.	all men with strong attachment to the mother become homosexual; Jones has a strong attachment to his mother; therefore Jones is homosexual.

In the example about spaniels the same true conclusion was derived by a valid argument on the one hand from false premises and on the other from true premises.

To say that something *e* is *an* explanation of something *h*, is to say only that *h* may be deduced by valid argument from *e*; it is not to say that the statements which make up *e* are true. This raises the very important question how the truth of the statements making up an explanation is to be established, for it is this which determines which explanation is correct.

CONFIRMATION OF EXPLANATION

An explanation (on the covering law model) will consist either of universal generalisations only, or of these together with statements about a particular situation (we shall not consider the role of definitions for the moment). Establishing the correctness of an explanation, then, will always require us to establish the truth of a universal generalisation, and will often involve us in establishing the truth of statements about particular situations. In cases where an explanation is given of a particular event, the truth of the particular facts making up the initial conditions is often not in doubt. There are, however, cases of this kind in which it is difficult to establish such facts. A psychologist, for example, might find it difficult to establish what the stimulus conditions for a group of rats in a maze are. Nevertheless, although it may be difficult to establish facts about the occurrence of particular events and the circumstances in which they occur, it is not in general or theoretically impossible to do so. Quite the reverse holds of the universal generalisations which occur in explanations. It is logically impossible to establish these by any form of investigation. Universal generalisations are assertions about infinitely large classes of events or things, and, since one cannot check an infinite number of cases, one cannot establish the truth of such assertions. Even such a proposition as "all crows are black" could not be established as true, for it is always possible that a white crow will be discovered in some remote place, or at some future time.

Could one not then say, if one knew that all crows now existing were black, that one could explain the blackness of a bird as follows:

(1) all present-day crows are black;
(2) this bird is a present-day crow;
(3) this bird is black ?

The objection to this is that (1) is not a universal generalis-ation; it is a generalisation about a finite or closed class, i.e., crows existing at a certain time and place. Other examples of this form would be the following:

(1) all men in this asylum now are mad;	(1) all the men in this room are under five feet in height;
(2) Jones is a man in this asylum;	(2) Jones is in this room;
(3) Jones is mad.	(3) Jones is under five feet in height.

These cases do not fit the covering law model, and one can see why they should be regarded as unsatisfactory. It is absurd to suggest that Jones is mad because he is in an asylum, or under five feet because he is in this room. Closed generalisations can often be established, but they are of limited usefulness. As soon as one has established their truth, one can no longer use them to explain, for they have no relevance to new events. If Jones is moved from this asylum, he may still be mad, but one can no longer apply the same generalisation to explain the madness; and the same is true of the other example. But something x cannot be the explanation of something y if y remains the same when x changes. In fact closed generalisations often represent quite fortuitous, or coincidental relationships.

Universal generalisations cannot be established. However, it is possible to test them; although they cannot be proved true, they can be proved false. No matter how many crows we examine and find to be black, it is still possible that there will be a white one one day. So the proposition "all crows are black" is never established beyond the possibility of correction. But if we find *one* white crow, we know that it is false. This is because the universal generalisation "all crows are black" entails that each crow is black, i.e. "if all crows are black then each crow is black" is logically true. Now if the consequent of a true hypothetical proposition is false, the antecedent must be false. But if we find one white crow it is false that each crow is black, hence that all crows are black. The technique then of testing universal generalisations is to attempt to falsify them; if they survive continuous testing of this kind, then we shall feel a certain confidence in them.

Since an explanation of the type we are considering must

contain a universal generalisation, the question whether it is correct or not depends on the question whether or not the universal generalisation in it is true or not. But a universal generalisation cannot be established except in the sense that it can be tested. It follows that the question whether an explanation of a particular event is correct or not cannot be answered by reference to the circumstances of that event alone. It will necessarily involve the further use of explanations of the same type in other cases. Any explanation of a particular event, in other words, has implications for similar events in the past and future. If we put forward such an explanation we are saying that the universal generalisation in it is true, and it follows that we are committed to predicting similar events in similar circumstances. For example, if I explain Jones's symptoms of measles as follows:

(1) anyone with bacterium x in the bloodstream develops spots;

(2) Jones has bacterium x in the bloodstream;

(3) Jones has spots;

I must agree that, if Smith has the bacterium x in his bloodstream, he too will show spots, and so on. But suppose that on some future occasion I predict, on the basis of the presence in his bloodstream of the bacterium x, that Smith will show spots, and he does not; in that case my universal generalisation will be falsified. This follows from the characteristics of valid arguments of which the prediction is an example:

(1) anyone with bacterium x in the bloodstream develops spots;

(2) Smith has bacterium x in the bloodstream;

(3) Smith develops spots.

If an argument is valid (as this one is) and its conclusion is false, it follows that one of its premises is false. In this case we take it for fact that Smith has bacterium x in the blood-stream. The universal generalisation, then, must be false. Now, since on this occasion it has been shown that the universal generalisation used in the prediction of Smith's symptoms is false, all the other explanations in which this generalisation was used must be regarded as incorrect; they too made use of this false generalisation.

The fact that an explanation appears to fit a given case very neatly does nothing at all to establish its correctness, not at least if the explanation is to be regarded as a scientific one. Such an explanation must be tested by the repeated application of explanations of the same kind to new cases. The pleasure felt by an investigator in finding an explanation which fits often leads him to forget that until many further tests have been made the explanation remains a mere suggestion, or hypothesis. It will be noticed that the covering law model of explanation makes explanation and prediction two sides of the same coin. Any explanation, since it includes a universal generalisation, can be applied to other objects, times and places, and if these are in the future, the explanation becomes a prediction.

FALSIFIABILITY

The view that universal generalisations, theories and explanations, can never be established, only shown to be wrong, leads to the formulation of a criterion for satisfactory explanations or theories, the criterion of falsifiability. In what follows I shall treat the testing of theories and universal generalisations in the same way, for a theory can be regarded as a set of universal generalisations related to one another in various ways, hence the use of a theory in explanation is formally similar to the use of a universal generalisation. We have seen that to test a theory, or universal generalisation, is to apply it to new cases by way of explanation or prediction. Testing a theory in this way is putting it at risk, and the risk arises because our predictions and explanations are logically rigorous deductions from premises which include the theory together with certain facts about a particular situation. The risk is that what is predicted or expected will not occur or be found: if that happens (and assuming that we have got our facts right), the theory must be rejected (as it stands; it may be reformulated). A theory can only be tested if it can be put at risk in this way. Now there are theories which, because of their character, or the way they are employed, cannot be put at risk. Theories of which this is true are unfalsifiable. But a theory which is unfalsifiable is unsatisfactory, for there is literally no means of testing, or confirming, its correctness. There are several ways in which a theory may be unfalsifiable or difficult to falsify, hence unsatisfactory.

Inconsistency. A theory may be self-inconsistent, that is, it may contain a group of propositions which, logically, cannot all be true. It is not always easy to detect such inconsistency, but its presence allows one to use the theory in such a way that it is never at risk. A very elementary example will illustrate this. It is an imaginary theory of a very simple kind consisting of three propositions as follows:

(1) all as are the same size as bs;
     all bs are of different size from as;
     all as are the same size as cs.

It is applied in particular circumstances described by (2)

(2) x is a c and y is a b;

to explain a particular fact described by (3):

(3) x is the same size as y.

The theory fits, for (3) follows from (2) and (1). But if the fact described by (3) had been exactly the opposite, that is (3)^1 "x is a different size from y", the theory would have fitted equally well, for (3)^1 also follows from (2) and (1). In other words, an inconsistent theory will fit any and every fact, and if we apply it in explaining facts, we shall never find any reason to reject it. If on the other hand the theory is used to make predictions, it is always possible that the wrong prediction will be made and the theory found to be false. Even when this happens, however, there is an enormous temptation not to reject the theory but to use it to explain the new fact. Thus one might say: "I used the theory to predict that an event x would occur, but y occurred. However the theory does predict the occurrence of y, so the prediction of x was a mistake". If the theory is sufficiently complex, and the calculations involved in making predictions allow some latitude, the inconsistency in the theory which makes these manœuvres possible may not be revealed.

Using a theory post hoc: one way of testing a theory is to apply it in explaining large numbers of cases. If a theory is consistent but incorrect, sooner or later some event will occur in such circumstances as to contradict the theory. But if a theory is inconsistent such a case need never arise, since by choosing this or that part of the theory one is able to make it fit any situation, and if one knows what the fact to be explained is one *can* choose the appropriate part of the theory. A second and further way of testing a theory is to predict what will occur in advance of the occurrence. Here again an incorrect but consistent theory is likely sooner or later to be proved false. An inconsistent theory is also likely to fail this kind of test. Of the two inconsistent parts of the theory only one will give the right prediction. But in predicting one is as likely to use one part as the other. This is one of the reasons why, in disciplines where there is some anxiety about whether or not a theory is consistent, great emphasis is rightly placed on testing the theory by prediction and not just by *post hoc* explanation of events, even large numbers of events.

Vagueness. If a theory is vague it is a matter of interpretation and personal decision whether or not the theory entails that a particular event will occur in certain circumstances. If the event fails to occur the theorist may simply reverse his decision and say that he misinterpreted the theory, or he may accuse others who use the theory of failing to interpet it correctly. Clearly, unless the procedure of deducing consequences from a theory is rigorously logical, it is impossible to regard any prediction as a test of the theory. The possibility of vagueness again emphasises the importance of using theories to predict, for whereas in *post hoc* explanation of events a theory can be interpreted so as to fit the event which has occurred, in prediction one at least risks choosing an interpretation which does not fit what subsequently happens, hence one risks predicting wrongly.

Tautology. Sometimes an hypothesis which looks like a factual generalisation is really a tautology, that is, its proponents are using the terms of the proposition so as to make it true by definition. Such an hypothesis is not refutable because it is trivially true. In a recent newspaper discussion on group violence a correspondent referred to a suggested explanation of group violence in terms of "group psychological intoxication". Presumably some such general-isation as "whenever there is group psychological intoxication there is group violence" lay behind the suggested explan-ation. One suspects, however, that this generalisation could never be falsified, since if there were no group violence it would doubtless be concluded that there was no group intoxication. In other words, it is difficult to imagine a way of establishing group intoxication which does not involve group violence. If in fact the term "group psychological intoxication" is really being used simply as another term for "group violence" then the generalisation is a tautology.

Scientific theories or hypotheses which are unfalsifiable, or untestable, are all unsatisfactory, not just because they are unfalsifiable, but because their unfalsifiability reflects their insulation from the world. The causes of unfalsifiability considered above, inconsistency, vagueness, tautology, all have this in common. The tautological hypothesis is insulated from facts about the world because the meaning of its terms makes it true. The inconsistent and vague theories are insulated from the world because they are compatible with any situation whatsoever. A theory which in effect fits all possibilities in the world of events tells us nothing about these events. Like the proposition "this is something", which also fits any situation, such theories convey no information.

AN EXPLANATION OF FORGETTING IN FREUD'S 'PSYCHOPATHOLOGY OF EVERYDAY LIFE'

In the *Psychopathology of Everyday Life* Freud gives explan-ations of a great variety of slips, errors and failures of memory. His explanation of one case of forgetting is worth examining closely since he gives it in some detail.

Freud begins by describing the circumstances in which

the forgetting occurred. He was travelling by train with a stranger between Ragusa in Dalmatia and a station in Herzegovina. The conversation turned to Italy, and Freud asked his companion if he had ever been in Orvieto and seen there the frescoes of ——. At this point he forgot the name of the painter, Signorelli, remembering only instead the names Botticelli and Boltraffio. Freud explained his lapse of memory as follows. Just before it he had been discussing the customs of the Turks living in Bosnia and Herzegovina and relating the reports of a medical colleague who quoted his patients as saying in response to gloomy prognoses, "Sir (Herr), what can I say? I know that if he could be saved you would save him". Freud had turned from this stream of thought and put it out of his mind for two reasons. First, there had been other reports from the colleague about the sexual attitudes of Turks, and these Freud would not have discussed with a stranger. Second, this train of ideas might have led him on to other matters associated with the theme of death and sexuality, in partic-ular the recent death by suicide of a former patient, news of which had reached him whilst in Trafoi.

The forgetting of "Signorelli" was due to its association with other matters which he wished to exclude from consciousness. These associative links are set out in the following diagram.

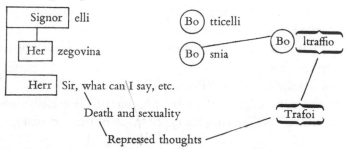

If someone claims to explain an event x by something y then he is implicitly asserting a universal generalisation connecting the two. We can therefore write out a full explanation of the forgetting of "Signorelli" as follows:

(1) if ever something x is repressed and something y is associated with x, then y is forgotten;

(2) the thoughts of death and sexuality were repressed and "Signorelli" was associated with them;

(3) "Signorelli" was forgotten.

However, it is to be noticed that the generalisation (1) could just as easily be used to predict the forgetting of "Boltraffio" and "Botticelli".

(1) if ever something x is repressed and something y is associated with x, then y is forgotten;

(2) the thoughts of death and sexuality were repressed and "Botticelli" and "Boltraffio" were associated with them;

(3) "Boltraffio" and "Botticelli" were forgotten.

But Freud recalled "Botticelli" and "Boltraffio", so given that the associations are correctly described, the universal generalisation must be false and the explanation of the forgetting of "Signorelli" incorrect. Freud in fact explains the remembering of "Boltraffio" and "Botticelli" as *substitutions* due to their association with the repressed thoughts of death and sexuality, and to complete *this* explanation we must express the universal generalisation implicit in it as follows:

(1) if ever something x is repressed and something y is associated with it, then y comes to mind;

(2) "Boltraffio" and "Botticelli" were associated with a repressed thought;

(3) "Boltraffio" and "Botticelli" came to mind.

Rather than recognise the remembering of "Botticelli" and "Boltraffio" as falsifying his explanation of the forgetting of

"Signorelli", Freud implicitly accepts two inconsistent universal generalisations. However, though in his explanations of remembering and forgetting these universal generalisations are implicit, since they are not both stated explicitly, the inconsistency is not immediately detectable.

Freud's explanation of these events also provides an excellent illustration of vagueness in theories, for the notion of association he uses is extremely imprecise. Almost anything *can* be regarded as associated with anything else. Given that most of us have some repressed thoughts, *any* case of forgetting could be attributed to association with a repressed thought. If the reader would like to perform an experiment let him substitute any sentence of his choice for the sentence, "Sir, what can I say, etc.", then attempt to connect it by associative links with "Signorelli" on the one hand and death and sexuality on the other. The exercise will make it clear how the flexibility of the notion of association allows any event to be explained by Freud's hypothesis.

CHAPTER 4

WHAT-EXPLANATIONS

SOMETIMES it is explanatory to say what something is, and to request an explanation is often to ask for no more than this sort of answer. Simple examples of this kind of explanation are easy to imagine. Can you explain what this is? It is a pea processing machine; it is a totem pole; it is the eye of a crab. Can you explain what is going on? It is a riot; the students are demonstrating against the war; the cell is dividing; the terms of trade are turning against us. Can you explain what he is doing? He is digging potatoes; he is conducting an imaginary orchestra; he is trying to cross the channel on foot. It would, however, be a mistake to think that what-explanations can be recognised by the verbal form of the question which they answer, for what-explanations can be given in answer to why-questions. For example, the answer "It's a riot", may be given to the question "Why are they running about shouting?"; the answer "They are in love", to "Why are they gazing at each other like that?"; the answer "It is dividing", to "Why is the cell changing shape?"

Some what-explanations are closely related to the activity of scientific explanation. A good part of the latter, as we have seen, consists in devising general theories and applying them to particular events. A scientific theory is often formulated in terms of behaviour of theoretical entities and to apply it in explanation of a particular event it is necessary to redescribe what was observed when the event took place using the terms of the theory. Thus to explain the behaviour of gases in terms of the kinetic theory it is necessary first to redescribe the gases as collections of molecules. To explain the behaviour of certain solids in terms of atomic theory it is necessary to redescribe them in terms of their atomic structure. Explaining what something is may in this way be a preliminary to scientific explanation. Even more closely linked with scientific explanation are some of the cases in which we explain what is going on. A scientific explanation consists in a deduction from premises which comprise universal generalisations and statements of circumstances. It is possible to give an explanation of what is going on which refers to such generalisations and statements of circumstances. For example, "the bodies are being attracted to one another with a force proportional to their mass and inversely proportional to the square of the distance between them", "the electrical current is breaking the water down into hydrogen and oxygen". Explanations of this kind are simply elliptical scientific explanations of events, the particular movements of certain bodies or the emission of hydrogen and oxygen from a liquid.

Whether or not and how far a what-explanation is related to a scientific explanation is a matter of whether or not and how far the redescription makes use of terms proper to a scientific theory, and, in the case of explanations of what is going on, of relationships which are expressed in the universal generalisations of that theory. This is not to say that no what-explanation can be related to scientific explanation unless there is already a well-formulated theory in the field. If, several hundred years ago, a man had been asked what was going on in a chemical reaction, and he replied that the materials were made up of a large number of tiny particles and that a rearrangement of these was taking place, he would, as it turns out, have been giving a what-explanation which was related to scientific explanation. However, to be *equivalent* to a scientific explanation an explanation of what is going on must either contain an elliptical reference to some known universal generalisation or imply the truth of some such generalisation, so as to allow its reformulation according to the covering law model. To say that a particular what-explanation *is related* to a scientific explanation is to say that it redescribes some thing or event in terms which can be employed in an explanation conforming to the covering law model.

It is often difficult to decide whether or not a given what-explanation is, or is meant to be, equivalent to a scientific explanation, and it may be even more difficult to decide whether or not it is related to a scientific explanation, that is, whether a scientific explanation can be formulated in the terms used. However, it is of great importance to be clear that there are a great many what-explanations whose explanatory character has nothing to do with the possibility either of reformulating them as scientific explanations, or of relating them to scientific explanations.

Suppose that Mrs Jones and I, on a walk in the country, observe Mr Jones and Miss Smith carrying a basket between them towards a wood. Mrs Jones asks me if I can explain what is going on. Now it may be that Mr Jones and Miss Smith are on their way to bury her recently dead pet (which is in the basket), or they may be taking food to the gypsies, or helping a business associate who is in hiding, or perhaps they are planning a surprise for Mrs Jones and myself. However, I may know enough to say that they are lovers going on a picnic. In saying so I give Mrs Jones an explanation of what is going on. For *her* the question how this came about, or whether such behaviour could have been predicted, is irrelevant. Simply knowing what Mr Jones and Miss Smith are doing is all that she requires of an explanation at this stage. Whereas before this she may have been unclear exactly how to describe what her husband was doing, she now knows. Moreover, knowing what she now knows, she will behave differently from the way she would have behaved had I said it was a pet's funeral or a mission of mercy. A comparable case is one in which a wife becomes puzzled by her husband's behaviour over a period of time. She goes to someone who explains that her husband no longer loves her but loves another woman. Now it all falls into place. His behaviour seemed to her puzzling in the light of her assumption that he loved her. When informed that he does not, she is no longer so puzzled. Again, I may sit down to eat what appears to be a lamb chop. I taste it and am puzzled because it seems wrong, and I ask my neighbour at the table to explain what it is. When he explains that it is a vegetarian groundnut steak my puzzlement is removed. These are cases where a thing or event appears to be an x but also displays properties incompatible with being an x; or cases where something could be one of a variety of things, only one cannot tell which from the immediate evidence.

From these examples and those earlier it emerges that one may have a variety of interests in what-explanations.

(1) There are what-explanations which are attempts to satisfy a theoretical or scientific interest. These explanations are redescriptions in terms which link the thing or event to scientific laws from which the event or the behaviour of the thing could be deduced, and future events or behaviour predicted. Such explanations may or may not have consequences for the actions of hearers.

(2) There are what-explanations which are not attempts to satisfy a theoretical interest but do supply information which satisfies our curiosity and which may affect practical decisions in ordinary life. People act in the light of circumstances as they perceive them; clarification of the circumstances can lead to modifications in their plans of action.

One of the problems about what-explanations is that they may very easily be thought to have a scientific interest when in fact they have not. Suppose that I am walking through the town with a friend and we observe people running about shouting and so on, and that he asks me to explain what is going on and that I reply that it is a battle between two religious sects; the explanation is quite satisfactory for his curiosity as to what is going on is satisfied. Moreover the information is of practical value; if I had said that there was an air-raid, or that an invasion was in progress our subsequent action would have been guided in a different way. However, if I have general beliefs about the kind of conditions under which religious riots occur, I may think that some such conditions prevailed. For example, that one side committed some act of injustice against the other, or that one side was planning the destruction of the other. If, in addition, I already know that the government is of one religious party and that it is pushing through legislation to suppress the other, I may think that I now know not just what is happening but why it is happening, that is, that I have something like a scientific explanation of the events. Furthermore, from my experience of religious riots I may form some view of what the outcome will be; I may make a prediction. However, in this case I will *not* have a scientific theory. I will have no knowledge of universal truths to enable me to deduce from the facts that the riot had to occur. Nor will I be able to predict with certainty that in these circumstances certain consequences must follow. We all have rough-and-ready theories about human behaviour and we may be tempted to think that whenever information about what is going on or what a thing is is explanatory, it is so because it enables us to apply our theories. If we find the information that something is a religious riot explanatory we may think that this can only be because it enables us to see how the riot came to occur. On the contrary: saying what something is can be explanatory, as I have suggested, whether or not the possibility of theorising or giving scientific explanations exists. In the field of human behaviour we often feel inclined to explain and our explanations are often regarded as acceptable. But the question must remain open whether these explanations are of a scientific kind—with all that this implies about the possibility of testing the explanations by deduction and prediction. The evidence at present suggests that they are not scientific.

A further problem is that some what-explanations employ generalisations and may therefore be mistaken for scientific explanations. This is the case with explanations in terms of economic models, or theories of political and social systems, for such models and systems are defined or characterised by interrelated generalisations or rules concerning the character of events and behaviour. Thus an explanation of the appointment of Harold Wilson as Prime Minister might take the following form:

(1) the British electoral system in the year 19— to 19— was such that, when x happened y happened, and if y was z, then a happened, while if y was w, then b happened, etc., etc.;

(2) in fact x happened, and y was w, so;

(3) b happened, i.e. Wilson was appointed.

(1) contains a number of generalisations and the event to be explained is deduced from it together with the facts in (2). Nevertheless explanations of this kind are not scientific. They employ generalisations solely in order to define a particular model or to characterise a particular system. Consequently the correctness of such an explanation depends only on whether that system or model obtained at the time of the event to be explained; it does not depend on the generalisations holding *universally*.

It would thus be possible to explain Wilson's appointment in terms of the system obtaining in the 1960s though this had changed since. Correspondingly if we predicted a future appointment on the basis of that system and were mistaken it would not follow that the original explanation was wrong, or that the generalisations concerned were false; they might have held then though not now; the system might have changed.

When an event is explained in terms of a social or economic system, no *universal generalisation* is actually asserted. Instead a system, in which events take place according to certain generalisations, is asserted to have obtained at a particular place and time. And this particular fact, like any other, requires scientific explanation.

It is useful here to compare an economic, or political, system with an electronic one, e.g. a radio. Both the proper and the faulty operation of a radio may be explained within the science of electronics. But there is as yet no body of laws which explains why a political, or economic, system holds at one time or breaks down at another. Thus, for example, there exists no general theory which would enable us to predict that in an election the returning officer, instead of declaring the winner elected, would shoot him.

Explanations in terms of models or systems then, consist only of particular statements of fact. They are explanatory because they describe patterns into which a particular event can be fitted. But they do not answer the scientific question why the event occurred for they do not explain why this system obtained and operated as it did.

To convert a what-explanation of this kind into a scientific explanation would require only that the system in question (and the generalisations, or principles defining it) be asserted to hold universally. But it seems that as yet no system, or model exists in the social sciences which is capable of such a universal application.

What-explanations tell us, or make clear to us, what something is or what is going on. In some cases such explanations are elliptical scientific explanations. When they are not, they may have a theoretical interest, or a practical interest, or they may simply convey more precise information to someone who does not know how to classify or describe something.

CHAPTER 5

EXPLANATIONS IN TERMS OF MENTAL STATES AND EVENTS

EXPLANATIONS in terms of mental states and events are common in ordinary life, in the courts, in history books, in novels and in criticism. Here are some simple examples:
- Why did his wife leave him? She hated the way he ate.
- Why did Jones kill the old lady? He wanted her money.
- Why did the vote for the National Socialist Party win increasing support from middle-class Germans during the 30s? They were distressed at the decline in their station during the depression years and they expected it to improve under Hitler.

There is a great variety of mental concepts. There are concepts of motive, intention, interest, desire, hope, expectation, belief, decision, mood, emotion, ability, knowledge and many others. Correspondingly there is a variety of explanations employing these concepts. Such explanations are clearly perfectly satisfactory; the question is how they are satisfactory, i.e. what kind of explanations they are.

In Chapter 6 I shall discuss the way in which a man's statements of his wants, attitudes and principles figure in reason-giving explanations. I shall argue that such statements are not to be interpreted as assertions of fact or as empirical hypotheses about his behaviour. However, most of the remarks we make about the mental states of others (not, for example, those which report a man's own reason-giving explanations) and many that we make about our own mental states are statements of fact. It is the role of *these* statements in explanation which I shall examine here; I shall refer to explanations in which they figure as 'mental concept explanations'.

The explanatoriness of mental concept explanations does not lie in implicit universal generalisations relating mental states to behaviour, for there are no such universal generalisations which have any plausibility. Compare the following explanations:

– Why did he kill her? He wanted her money.
– Why did the apple fall? The stem was cut.

A contrast is apparent as soon as one asks what connects the two facts mentioned in each example. The fall of the apple and the cutting of the apple stem are clearly related by some universal generalisation about gravity, but no such relationship holds between wanting someone's money and killing them. The relation between these is not only not universal, it is not even common.

But it might be argued that the first example is formulated unsatisfactorily—there *is* a universal generalisation implicit in the explanation, but the mental condition and the circumstances of its occurrence need to be described in more detail if a plausible generalisation connecting them is to be formulated. On this view the difference between the two examples above is only apparent; they are really both instances of scientific explanation. The fact is, however, that on the one hand the example does seem to be, and would be generally accepted as, explanatory as it is (and in a particular case it might be regarded as the correct explanation); on the other hand, no universal proposition, however elaborate, relating mental states such as desires or wants to such actions as killings could even be entertained as probable let alone true. It seems clear that in giving explanations of this type one does not intend to imply the truth of any universal generalisation. If one did all one's explanations of this kind would be incorrect. These explanations are acceptable as explanations but they do not fit the scientific model. If there is any doubt in the reader's mind about this he should try to imagine universal propositions relating mental states to action. He will not discover any which he cannot show immediately to be false.

Mental states are not mental causes of physical events (behaviour). To suggest that physical movements, which are changes in the electrical, chemical, and physical properties of cells, could be due to non-physical states or events is to suggest, in fact, that theories within the sciences of chemistry, electronics and physics are all false. These theories acknowledge no way in which changes in chemical, electrical or physical states can occur except as a result of changes in other chemical, electrical, or physical parameters. Yet to attribute physical effects to mental (i.e. non-physical) causes is to deny this and to assert that some chemical, electrical, and physical changes have causes of quite a different kind.

A further objection to this view is that it involves treating mental states and events as similar in certain ways to physical events and states. In particular, if mental states and events are to be related to behaviour as causes of it, they must occur at specific times and last for specific periods of time in the way that physical events and states do. But physical and mental states and events are not alike in this respect. Compare, for example, the state of knowing French and the state of being magnetised. One can ask whether a thing was magnetic between 10.00 and 10.30, or 10.29 and 10.30, but it does not make sense to ask of someone who knows French whether he knew it between 10.29 and 10.30, or at 10.15 precisely. Similar difficulties crop up with other mental states. A man may have wanted a Rolls-Royce all his life, but it does not follow that at 2.00 p.m. yesterday he wanted one. Whereas to be magnetic over a period is to be magnetic at each instant of it, wanting a Rolls all one's life does not imply wanting it at every instant of every day.

Explanations and predictions of the following forms

(1) A wanted x;   (1)^1 A wants x;

(2) doing y was going to get   (2)^1 doing y will gain him x;
     him x;

(3) so A did y.   (3)^1 A will do y.

seem to mention facts which tell us how A's action y came about or enable us to predict A's action in the way that a scientific explanation or prediction would. But in neither case do (1) and (2) entail (3). It would have been perfectly possible for (1) and (2) to be true and (3) false, and it is possible for (1)^1 (2)^1 to be true and (3)^1 to turn out false.

There does appear, however, to be a connection between, for example, wanting money and killing the possessor of money, hating someone and leaving them, expecting something from someone and voting for them, wanting something and doing what is necessary to get it; and the connection seems to be stronger than mere correlation. The nature of the connection appears to be this: quite a large number of mental concepts themselves refer to behaviour, so that statements employing them are in turn about behaviour. Mental concepts of which this seems to be true are those which relate to capacities, and tendencies such as knowledge, emotion, mood, desire, interest and belief. Concepts of which it is least likely to be correct are those which relate to sensations. Other concepts, such as intention, are difficult even to begin to classify. The main problem here, however, is to explain *in what way* mental concepts of the first class refer to behaviour.

It might be suggested that mental concepts can be defined in terms of behaviour. One might say, for example, that hitting someone was part of the definition of what it is to be angry, or that making efforts to get something was part of the definition of wanting things of that type. If this were right, however, one could not say of a person that he was angry if he did not hit someone; hitting someone would become a necessary condition of being angry. But it seems that no particular kinds of behaviour are connected in *this* way with mental states and events. There are no particular bits of behaviour which invariably accompany a given mental state. Moreover there would be something absurd in explaining hitting by the state of anger if these were definitionally connected; it would be like explaining why someone was male by saying that he was a brother.

Another suggestion about the relationship between mental concepts and behaviour is that mental concepts refer not to behaviour as such but to *dispositions* to behave in certain ways. One might distinguish two kinds of dispositions: tendencies, such as being generous or irritable, and capacities, such as knowing French. On this account mental-concept statements are to be interpreted as hypothetical propositions about how a person behaves in certain circumstances. This is attractive since it allows us to say that a mental concept refers to behaviour without requiring us to say that a person in a certain mental state must be behaving in a certain way at any particular time. It need only be true that *if* certain things happen he will behave in certain ways. To take an example which seems to fit the theory: it seems reasonable to say that the statement that a person knows French simply means that if certain circumstances arise he will speak French or write in French or react appropriately to speech or writing in the language. The statement certainly does not imply that he is acting in some special or relevant way at this particular moment.

But there are difficulties lurking beneath these apparently straightforward suggestions. When we speak of something having a disposition we mean not just that in a given situation it will behave in a certain way but also that if it were in such a situation it would behave in this way (even if the situation has never, in fact, arisen). Thus, to say that a lump of sugar is soluble is to say that if it were put in water it would dissolve. Propositions about what would have happened if something had occurred (counter-factual hypotheticals) are extremely difficult to understand, in that one cannot say just what it is that leads one to think some of them true and others false. With this difficulty unsolved dispositional accounts of mental concepts are in a sense incomplete: we do not fully understand what is involved in them.

There is a further difficulty. Whereas certain physical states can be defined in terms of reactions in a particular test situation (for example, to say that something is magnetic is to say that if certain tests are performed on it certain results will be obtained), the same is not true of mental states. It is possible to regard magnetism as a disposition (a tendency, or capacity) because it is possible to formulate hypothetical propositions of the form "if x is done, reaction y will occur" which express what we mean by calling something magnetic. It is tempting to suppose that the same is true of mental states such as anger, knowing French and being intelligent, but it is not. If a person is angry, or knows French, one certainly expects that if certain things happen, he will behave in certain ways, but it is not possible to formulate one's expectations as precise hypothetical propositions which are always true of someone in one of these states. Must it be true that if a person knows French and is spoken to in French, he will answer in French? Clearly not. If his life depends on it will he speak French? Not necessarily. One cannot devise a test situation in which a man who knows French must behave in a specific way.

A simpler form of behaviourism is the view that mental concepts refer not to dispositions but to actual behaviour. The difficulty here has always been that, as we saw earlier, no particular behaviour is essential to any given mental state. In the extreme case a man might be angry and yet conceal it completely. It is possible, nevertheless, that mental concepts do refer to behaviour, not to *particular bits of behaviour* like hitting and kissing, but to *patterns* of behaviour. The word "chair" does not refer to any particular shape of wood, nor indeed to any particular kind of material, nor can it be defined in terms of such elements. Nevertheless chairs are arrangements of pieces of wood or other material of various shapes; and tables are arrangements of a different kind. Chairs vary enormously in the materials from which they are made and in the shape and arrangement of their parts. So also do tables. Yet we are able to distinguish tables from chairs. Similarly the behaviour which we call anger is made up of many different particular acts arranged in various ways; so also is the behaviour we call love. Yet, of course, we are able to distinguish love from anger.

To say that mental states are patterns of behaviour still leaves us with the difficult problem of how one decides in a particular case which pattern of behaviour one is confronted by. In judging a person to be angry, or in love, to intend this, or want that, one usually observes some element of the situation and of his behaviour and then makes a guess or judgement as to how his behaviour will develop just as after seeing only a part of a piece of furniture we may say, "It's a chair". But of course in both cases we can be wrong. And the problem is much harder with behaviour than it is with furniture. When judging behaviour one has to *wait* for things to develop, and there are complex relationships between behaviour and situation to assess. At any given moment several views about the pattern may seem equally possible (love or hate, love or respect, love or infatuation, love or lust) and it may require the intervention of an observer to initiate behaviour which resolves the uncertainty. Certain sorts of mental statements are easier to verify than others. Mental statements about capacities, such as knowing French or the way to Oxford, can at least be judged true if the person about whom the statement is made actually utters some French or finds his way to Oxford. (They are more difficult to prove false.) Statements about a person's emotions, moods, attitudes, feelings or desires, are much more difficult. There seems no specific behaviour which would *either* show them true, *or* show them false. The pattern one discerns may vary from time to time and one may never be certain what to say. It is tempting to think in these cases that there is a real truth which we are bound to discover if we do enough research. But, in fact, as we shall see in the chapters on explanation in literature and history, there is no sense in which a person must *really* be either in love or infatuated, *really* intend this or that. The reality is the behaviour; the pattern is what we make of it.

Since different people are likely to see different patterns it is never possible to say with finality about mental statements of this type that one is true or another false. The same is true of our judgements about ourselves the only difference being that we know more about our own behaviour than others do, e.g. we know the things we say to ourselves.

To explain a particular action by mentioning a mental state such as anger is to characterise that action as part of a pattern of behaviour, one of the patterns of behaviour we call anger. Why is it explanatory to be told that a particular action is part of a pattern of action? Because then we know what is going on. Suppose I find a girl weeping—there are an enormous number of behaviour patterns of which her weeping could be a part. She could be peeling onions, jilted in love, acting, suffering from a disease, hysterical, or miserable. Being told which it is will not inform me exactly what she will do next, nor exactly what has happened to her, any more than telling me that something is a chair informs me exactly how it is made or of what. But I will know roughly what sort of thing to expect and what sort of thing has probably happened. To take another example: if I were asked why Jones hit Smith I might say that he was angry. In this way, I should be distinguishing a pattern of behaviour from other patterns such, for example, as would be described by saying that Jones had mistaken Smith for another man, or that he was revenging himself, or that he was acting in a film, or that he was sparring, or that it was a twitch.

Mental-concept explanations are what-explanations. They tell us what sort of pattern a particular event or piece of behaviour is a part of. They are not normally explanations which could be re-formulated as attempts at scientific explanation, for they are not attempts to relate two things in such a way that one could be predicted from the other. Just as in explaining an object by saying that it is a part of a chair, one is not mentioning a fact from which it would be possible to deduce that it is as it is (e.g. of this shape or that size), or show how it came to be as it is, so in explaining a piece of behaviour by saying that a person is angry, one is not mentioning something from which the behaviour could have been deduced, nor something which explains how the behaviour came about.

It is possible that the patterns which we pick out when we attribute mental states will achieve recognition in the descriptive terminology of some future science of psychology. Indeed in the field of personality theory attempts are already being made to devise precise ways of measuring such characteristics as generosity, egocentricity, anxiety, depression, intelligence, and so on. And in behaviour theory we find states which resemble e.g. a desire, or knowledge, or a mood figuring as intervening variables. Such attempts to carry the concepts of ordinary language into psychology involve not just clarification but re-definition. However, whether or not such revised mental concepts will be of use in the scientific explanation of behaviour must depend upon the possibility of discovering the necessary universal generalisations relating ratings on these new measures to specific behaviour. At present one must regard everyday explanations employing mental concepts as having a practical but not a theoretical interest. Despite our inclination to believe that we have considerable understanding of the behaviour of others, and that we know all sorts of general truths about the way people behave, we are in fact constantly mistaken in our judgements about them. Nor is this less true of our judgements about ourselves.

CHAPTER 6

REASONS

ASKING and answering why in relation to human behaviour is often quite unlike asking for and receiving a scientific explanation. The difference can be indicated very easily by examples. If I am asked why I believe that there is a god I may reply in two quite different ways.

(1) I may refer to what I, as a naive scientist of human nature (a naive psychologist), take to be the causes of my holding this belief—for example, that I was brought up in this faith, that my family mixed only with religious people, or that I met a man who converted me when I was seventeen. To explain in this way is to treat holding the belief as a fact about me like my height or my character and to suggest the scientific principles in accordance with which I came to be this way.

(2) I may quote evidence in support of my belief and give my reasons for holding the belief—for example, the apparently extraordinary facts of the life of Jesus, the necessity for life having a purpose, the necessity for the world having had a creator, etc. Here I give arguments which are supposed to show that holding the belief is warranted, justifiable, or acceptable.

I may, also explain my actions in two ways, e.g. how I vote.

(1) I may refer to my upbringing in a politically committed family, or to social and economic determinants of my behaviour, implying that empirical laws relate these factors to voting behaviour.

(2) On the other hand I may assert Labour's policy to be

the right one, referring to my experience of its effects as evidence, or mention my debt to the party for its services, or my duty to vote in the same way as my workmates. Here I try to show that my action conformed with what I believed to be right.

Explanations of the second kind I shall call reason-giving explanations. They show why an action or belief is (or was) thought to be (or to have been) a good thing to do, right, correct, or true (or some other of a long list of commend-atory terms). They explain why something is happening or happened, only in the sense that they show why it is or was thought a good thing to do, or the correct thing to believe.

GIVING A REASON

We give reasons to explain both why we did something and why we are doing or will do something. We also give them in advising others how to act, in deciding our own course of action and as a contribution to public deliberation.

I shall begin with examples in which a man explains why he is doing something:

– A: (1) Why are you going to the United States of America?
– B: (2) There is a conference on there.

What B gives as his reason, namely (2), is a statement of fact. But this fact cannot explain his journey, unless it is assumed to have a special relevance to his decision to go, as would be the case if e.g. he felt under an obligation to attend the conference or particularly wanted to be present. Nor would we describe his reply as giving a reason for his journey except on such an assumption.

– B: (3) I am going to give ten pounds to Oxfam.
– A: (4) Why?

– *B*: (5) Ten pounds for Oxfam will help alleviate suffering in Africa.

Again *B*s statement can be described as 'giving a reason' only if there is a special connection between it and his action, for example that he cannot bear reading the news reports from Africa, or that he holds it a moral duty to assist in the alleviation of suffering.

In each case *B* explains his proposed action by mentioning what he takes to be a fact. But his explanations are elliptical. To complete them he must make explicit what is implied, namely that he wants, or thinks himself under an obligation, or feels morally bound, to do something which, if his belief is correct, his proposed action will accomplish. These implied wants, obligations and moral principles I shall call relating factors to distinguish them from the other aspect of *B*s explanations, his beliefs as to the facts.

Sometimes, requests for reasons are met by explicit reference to a relating factor while the beliefs of fact are left to be inferred. For example, instead of (2) *B* might have replied:

– $(2)^1$ I want to go to a conference

and instead of (5);

– $(5)^1$ One ought to do what one can to relieve suffering.

He must in this case be presumed to hold some such belief as (2) or (5).

Giving reasons for action then is complex involving both beliefs about facts and relating factors. And sometimes this complexity is apparent when a man in giving his reason mentions both explicitly.

Explanations of beliefs are similarly complex,

– *A*: Why do you think the answer to the problem "$y + 3 = 7 - x$, find y", is 4?

- *B*: $x=0$, so by the rules of algebra $y=4$.
- *A*: Why do you think Jones is in Oxford?
- *B*: He must be either in Oxford or London and he is not in London, so by logic he is in Oxford.
- *A*: Why do you think Jones is in Oxford?
- *B*: Several people report seeing him there and their reports constitute evidence.
- *A*: Why do you believe the picture to be by Rembrandt?
- *B*: Professor Smith says it is and he is an acknowledged expert.

In each case there is a relating factor, a rule of inference or calculation is cited, or an opinion about evidence or expertise is expressed, and there are beliefs or premises concerning the facts.

The seeming variety of these relating factors, in the case of actions, wants, moral principles and obligations, in the case of beliefs, rules of correct calculation and inference and opinions concerning evidence or authority, poses a question. Is there anything which warrants us in lumping them together and regarding explanations in which they figure as similar? There is; relating factors are all concerned with evaluation. They are views about what makes, or makes it likely that, something is good, a good thing to do, right, correct, true, proper, satisfactory, or nice, etc. They are all expressions of evaluative views.

Evidence for a belief supports it; an expert's judgements are likely to be correct; the rules of logic and algebra are principles of correct inference and computation; a moral principle is a view as to which actions are right; an obligation is something one ought to perform. It is less obvious that our statements of wants and wishes express evaluative views. Nevertheless to want to do something of a certain kind x is certainly to think x a good, or at least nice thing to do, though not necessarily good or nice for everyone. Indeed statements of wishes and wants *must* express views about the value of actions, for deciding on the best course often consists simply in choosing between, or attempting to accommodate, conflicting wants. When wants conflict with obligations or principles it is because both are seen as relevant to the same issue; what is the best thing to do. One might say, for example, "I want to please my wife, but I ought not to indulge her. What is the best thing to do?", or "Some want to go to London, others to Liverpool, the best thing to do is to take in both cities on the outing", or "We all want to go on holiday and we have no conflicting obligations at the moment so the best thing to do is to set off now".

Reasons for beliefs and actions are in fact considerations which bear upon the relative goodness of courses of action or the relative correctness of beliefs; the beliefs of fact because they relate the possible action or belief to an evaluative view, the relating factors because they are evaluative views. To explain a particular action or belief by giving one's reason is always to say why one thinks or thought the action a good thing to do or the belief correct.

Thus the form of reason-giving explanation of a past action x would be as follows:

(1) I (He) held it right, or good, or nice, to do things of type y. Moreover

(2) I (He) believed doing x to be a case of doing y. So

(3) I (He) reckoned x a good thing to do (or right or nice).

Which is why

(4) I (He) did x.

Notice that while the view expressed in (3) is a deduction from the beliefs and opinions expressed in (1) and (2), the fact stated in (4) is not deducible from them. This type of explanation does not entail what it explains.

HAVING A REASON AND BEING A REASON

Whether, when a man gives something as his reason, he is properly said to have this reason is a matter of what beliefs and views he holds. This is a question of fact about him. No matter how bizarre the beliefs or views he expresses in giving his reason, if he has them (or thinks he does) he would be correctly described as having this reason for his action. Disagreement with a man's value views is not, therefore, a ground for denying that he has a reason for his actions. (One might comment instead, to take an example, "He has a reason for refusing to join the Army for he believes killing to be wrong, but I do not, so I have not".) But one may concede that someone has a reason for doing y, namely x, yet deny that x is a reason for doing y, for whether a fact x is in general a reason for doing something y is an evaluative issue to which people holding different evaluative views must give different answers. If I know that A has views about the goodness of doing x and that y is a case of x, I must agree that *he has a reason* for doing y. But if I do not accept his views I cannot agree that *x is a reason* for doing y; to concede this would imply that I too thought x a good thing which I do not.

Even if I agree with A's evaluative views and acknowledge his reasons as reasons I may yet dispute the relative importance he attaches to different reasons. What he calls a good reason I may count a bad one. I accept it as a reason but give it little weight.

THE CORRECT REASON-GIVING EXPLANATION

A man might have several possible reasons for an action any of which would explain it. To give *the* explanation is to select one of these as *his* reason for his action, or *the* reason why he did it. How, then, are we to determine what his reason for a particular action was, or the reason why he did it? There are two aspects to the question; how do we determine that he had a particular reason, and how do we know this to be his reason for doing what he did? I shall argue that both these questions can be answered only by reference to what a man says.

THE REASON WHY

The sentences "The reason why I did x was y" and "The reason why he did x was y" are highly ambiguous. Someone may use the first to give his reason for doing x and I may use the second to report it. Both these would be reason-giving explanations. But the sentences may also be used to suggest scientific explanations, for example, "The reason why I fell was that I was pushed", or "The reason why the car crashed was that the tyres were bald", and what-explanations, for example, "The reason why the truck is in Jerusalem is that it is en route from Bagdad to Haifa".

The expression "his reason for—", on the other hand, seems to have only one use, namely to introduce or refer to a reason-giving explanation.

HIS REASON FOR DOING X IS (OR WAS) Y

A man's reason for his action is the reason he sincerely gives (or gave). He may speak of 'his reason', or of 'the reason why he acted', or simply say he did it 'because of' such and such.

But whichever form he uses, if he gives a particular reason and gives it sincerely, it *is* his reason.

Other expressions resemble "his reason" in this respect:
- His explanation is the one he gives.
- His account is the one he gives.
- His defence is the one he pleads.
- His excuse is the one he offers.

To report a man's explanation, account, or excuse is to report what he said usually in indirect speech, e.g. "His excuse was that his mother was ill". Similarly in "His reason for not praising the child was that God would inflict some evil on him if he did", the word "that" signals a report in indirect speech.

But accounts are different from defences and reasons. Brown's account may be contrasted with the true one while there is no corresponding contrast either between Brown's defence and the true defence, or between Brown's reason and the true or correct reason for his action. Again reasons differ from defences and excuses, for what a man gives as his reason is only his reason if it is given sincerely.

Why should a man's reason be what he says (or says sincerely) it is? What gives his sincere explanation of his action such authority? We should not concede a special status to a man's scientific explanation of his behaviour; why then to his reason-giving explanation? I shall suggest two reasons.

(1) I argued that to give one's reason for an action is to explain why one thinks or thought it a good thing to do (or the best thing to do, etc.), that is, to make clear the reasoning which led to the decision to do it. Thus when Brown, explaining a past action, says "I married Mabel because she had long hair and because I wanted a wife with

long hair", he recalls what led him to think it a good idea to marry Mabel.

The 'because' in this explanation is easily confused with the 'because' in "she fell because she was pushed", or "the car skidded because the tyres were bald" where it refers to a causal relation. In Brown's reason-giving explanation it expresses the quite different relationship of ground to inference, premise to conclusion, (as e.g. in "I infer he's out because he's either in or out and he's not in"). The difference can be simply demonstrated. If it is false that Mabel was pushed, then it is false that she fell because she was pushed. Similarly if the tyres were not bald, then the car did not crash because of bald tyres. But if it turns out that Mabel had short hair, or if Brown becomes convinced that he didn't really want to marry long hair, it nevertheless remains true that he married Mabel because she had long hair so long as, at the time, he thought she had long hair and that he wanted a long-haired wife. His explanation consists not in asserting that what he thought was true but in recounting what he thought. It may be re-expressed without change of meaning to make this explicit:

– I married Mabel because I thought she had long hair and because I thought I wanted a long-haired wife.

In this form it is clear that it is irrelevant whether what Brown thought was true.

It might be objected that this is not just a different way of expressing the same explanation but a change of explanation. What was in fact a causal explanation relating facts about Mabel's hair and Brown's wants to a particular action has been replaced by a different causal explanation of the same action in terms of facts about Brown's thoughts. The objection, however, fails. Although Brown married Mabel because he thought her hair long, his reason for marrying her was not the nature of his thoughts but the nature (as he supposed) of her hair. His explanation may be re-written yet again:

– I thought that it was a good idea to marry Mabel because of her long hair and my desire for a long-haired wife.

What follows the word "that" in this last formulation is a report of Brown's deliberations. He took certain things for granted and on that basis came to a decision about the best course of action. His explanation is not a causal hypothesis, of the form "I had thought p because I had thought q", but a report of reasoning, of the form "I thought 'p because q'".

A man who gives x as his reason for doing y reports, or recalls that he thinks, or thought y a good thing to do because of x. Whether x is, or was his reason then, depends on whether he has or had these thoughts. But to speak sincerely is to say what one thinks. Consequently if someone reports his thoughts sincerely, he has or had those thoughts.

Now this relationship between sincere report and truth does not provide a means of testing reports, for whether a man speaks sincerely is just as difficult a question as whether he has the thoughts he claims to have. But it does reflect the fact that a man speaks with a special authority about his thoughts which he does not possess when he ventures on a scientific explanation of his behaviour. Of course a person might remember incorrectly, but how could he be wrong about what he thought when he thought it? This would be to suggest that he might think he thought x yet wonder whether he was right, and that he might investigate the matter. And this surely implies the absurdity that he might have thoughts of which he was unaware.

We may of course doubt a man's sincerity and suspect him of trying to deceive us as to his reasons. We may, for example, think that he is concealing another reason for his action. Now if on another occasion he gives a different reason, as we believe sincerely, we may call it his real reason to distinguish it from his earlier explanation. But if he does not, a reason-giving explanation is excluded, since there is nothing we can call 'his reason', the reason he sincerely gave. To pursue the question we must ask instead for the reason why he acted and, as we shall see, for a different kind of explanation.

The situation is the same if we suspect a man of deception, though not of concealing another reason. He may not know why he acted as he did though he tries to make us believe he does. Since in this case he has no reason for his action, no reason-giving explanation is possible. Once again if an explanation is demanded, it must be of some other kind.

But, it might be urged, granted the reason a man gives sincerely *is* his reason, why should we not conjecture someone's reasons for an action, either when he gives none, or when we suspect deceit? Why should it be a necessary condition of something being A's reason that he gives it as his reason? To answer this question I turn to a second reason for treating what a man says as crucial in determining his reasons.

(2) Consider the following argument: people often think they want something x when it is clear from their behaviour that they really want y. Thus a man might think and say sincerely that he wants medical advice when in fact he wants attention, or that he holds all killing to be immoral when his real concern is for his immediate family. One may mistake

the desire to ascend the social scale for the desire to move house, or fear of one's father for respect. In such a case a man may judge, because he thinks he wants x, that y is the best thing to do, hence he will, rightly, give this as his reason for doing y. But the true explanation of his action will lie elsewhere since he does not want what he says he wants, or hold what he says he holds.

The argument is designed to show not that a man's reason-giving explanations of his actions may be wrong, i.e. inaccurate reports of his thoughts or reasoning, but that though sincere they may yet simply reflect his illusions about himself. They should be replaced not by a different account of his reasoning but by a different type of explanation, in terms of his real wants, etc. Its conclusion is that reason-giving explanations are in general suspect. The extent to which people's reasons for their actions reveal anything more than their illusions can be discovered only by determining their wants, beliefs and principles of conduct by an empirical investigation of their behaviour. The conclusion, however, is unsound; it rests on a mistaken view of the nature of statements of wants and principles in reason-giving explanations.

A man may make statements about his wants or principles based on observations of his own behaviour. But when he gives his reason for an action he does not make a statement about them, he *states* them. To state one's wants, principles or beliefs is not to make a statement about, or to reflect publicly upon, one's behaviour, it is to subscribe to, to reaffirm, or to announce one's adoption of a way of behaving; to express, or reveal the intention to behave in a certain way. It would be bizarre replying to the question "Why are you proposing to me?" to say, reflecting on one's behaviour, "It seems as far as I can judge, from my own observations and those of others, that I want to marry you". What is required of the suitor is not a statement about his apparent wants but an announcement of his intentions, a readiness to commit himself to the view that the marriage is a good idea.

I argued earlier that for a man to have x as a reason for doing y he must have some want or hold some principle; he must have certain evaluative views. This is not to say that he must behave or believe that he is behaving in a particular way, for the views a man holds, or subscribes to, are not deducible from his behaviour; what views he holds is not a matter of how he behaves. On the one hand, because his statements of wants, principles, etc., often express intentions, his past behaviour may be a poor guide, or no guide at all to their truth. They may express past intentions to which he has failed to adhere, or wants and principles which he has only recently adopted. On the other hand what a man subscribes to and what he does are really quite different issues. Someone might behave in accordance with a particular desire or principle and know this, yet not subscribe to it (if for example he had a compulsive desire, or a habit he could not break). Although his behaviour was in accord with his holding x a good thing to do, if he did not subscribe to that opinion it would be wrong to say that he held it. A man may be regarded as committed to a particular evaluative view only if he declares it to be his view. Hence *his* statements alone justify the ascription of evaluative opinions to him.

Freedom to announce or reveal one's evaluative views is not a liberty to make true by stating it what may in fact be false. Such announcements and revelations are not reflections on the facts of one's behaviour; indeed they are not factual statements at all. However they do express commitment to a course of action consistent with the desire or principle in question, so that a man must take care what he says for fear of the criticism and reproach which will attend if he fails to act appropriately.

A man's wants or principles, like his intentions, are what he sincerely states them to be, or to have been (putting aside failures of memory). The charge "That's not true", in reply to such a declaration (whether past or present), is not an accusation of error but of deceit. Only if it became impossible to take a person's expressions of intention seriously as a guide to his behaviour could reason-giving explanations be regarded as suspect. In this case rather than calling such explanations illusory we should abandon them altogether, as we should abandon the practice of promising if no one ever kept his promise.

THE FUNCTIONS OF REASON-GIVING

What is achieved by an explanation depends on the kind of explanation it is. Reason-giving explanation requires us to reveal the beliefs and evaluative views which led us to think a particular action a good thing to do, or a particular belief correct. Consequently its function will be to do whatever may be achieved by such revelations.

(1) Where several people hold similar views as to what is good or correct one of them may, by giving his reasons for doing it (e.g. by citing facts), convince the others of the satisfactoriness or superiority of a particular course of action.

(2) A man may explain his own present or past actions hoping that those to whom he speaks, having similar views,

will agree that his actions are, or were, right, or at least unobjectionable.

(3) Conceding his action to be or to have been wrong, or bad, or unsatisfactory (because, for example, he made a mistake or had the facts wrong) a man may nevertheless hope to persuade men of similar evaluative views that his aim was reasonable, or that his intentions were good. His action may then appear justified.

(4) Where there is disagreement about what is good or right there may yet be a common view as to the relative importance of different types of reasons (e.g. that moral principles weigh more than personal wants and both more than the voice of authority). By explaining his actions a man may show at least that he has the right sense of priorities ("He has the strangest moral views but he governs his life by them") and in this way gain a measure of approval.

(5) Finally, a man who gives his reason for acting, if he accomplishes no more, reveals something of himself, what he thinks or feels to be good, right or important. If one half of the desire to be understood by others is the hope of justifying one's actions, the other is the hope of sympathy. Much of our assessment of others is based upon the reasons they give for their actions, or their lack of reasons. In explaining why he believed that p, or thought q correct a man may reveal himself as gullible or hard-headed, illogical or logical, slapdash or methodical. In explaining why he thought a picture good he may, in our judgement, show himself to be sophisticated or naive, sensitive or insensitive. And in explaining his actions a man, by revealing his wants and principles, lays himself open to judgement as normal or abnormal, natural or unnatural, steady or erratic, sympa-

thetic or unsympathetic, rational or irrational, moral or immoral, etc.

One who beats his wife because he finds it pleasurable may seem more agreeable than one who does it from a sense of duty. Similarly one who beats his children because he cannot bear their screams may attract more sympathy than one who believes a beating does them good. Whether he acted rightly or was justified in acting as he did is only a part of the assessment we make of a man and his actions from his own explanations.

REASONS AND SCIENTIFIC EXPLANATION

One view of the relationship between scientific explanation and explanations in terms of reasons is that they are incompatible. Thus Collingwood and, more recently, Winch, have argued that it is impossible to apply the methods of scientific observation and explanation to human behaviour.

In *The Idea of History* Collingwood draws a sharp distinction between history and science. The concern of history, he maintains is to explain actions, that of science to explain events. Now events are the product of causes operating in accordance with laws of nature while actions are decided on for reasons. Consequently the explanations of actions and events will be quite different.

In our everyday explanations of human behaviour we do in fact distinguish between reasons and causes. But this distinction corresponds neither to that between actions and events, nor to that between reason-giving and scientific explanation. Actions may in fact be explained both by reasons and by causes. Which of these is appropriate in a particular case is a matter of the circumstances (including the thoughts, feelings and attitudes of the participants) in which the action takes place. When a man does something because it seems a good idea to do it, we speak of reasons. On the other hand if he does something because he can't help it (e.g. he is subject to intolerable pressure, or overwhelming temptation) or he fails to act due to circumstances beyond his control, we speak instead of causes. Thus if Jones acts rudely at a party the explanation might lie in a reason, e.g. he wished to insult one of the guests, or in a cause, e.g. he could not bear the company. In both cases we explain an action, and in neither case is our explanation scientific.

In fact reason-giving and scientific explanations seems less to exclude one another than to provide answers to different questions; why did action x seem a good idea to A? and, why did x in fact happen? Consequently there seems no reason why a particular action should not receive both kinds of explanation. Indeed it seems that it must. A reason-giving explanation of A's action x only shows why A thought it a good idea to do x. It leaves unanswered the further question, why A in fact did what he thought it would be a good idea to do. Even if A had believed x to be the best possible course, he might not have taken it. He might have changed his mind, or acted differently on an impulse, or been prevented from doing x. A man's thoughts as to the value of doing something x do not entail his doing x, hence they cannot explain why x in fact happened. This is the province of scientific explanation.

It might be objected that an explanation deals with what happened, not with what might have happened. Thus given A did not act impulsively and was not prevented from doing x etc., given in effect that he did x, his reasons provide a full explanation of his action. The same argument may be applied to the explanation of a physical event. The fact that a seed fell in a pot cannot by itself explain why it grew there; other conditions are required for growth. But given that the seed grew, the fact that it fell in the pot is a sufficient explanation of its growing there. Now the form of such an 'explanation' is as follows:

(1) x grew;

(2) x was in the pot;

(3) x grew in the pot.

But (1) and (2) together simply mean the same as (3) hence they cannot explain the fact stated in (3).

Similarly the claim that, given A did x, the fact that he thought x the best thing to do explains his action, may be represented as follows:

(1) A did x;

(2) A thought x was the best thing to do;

(3) A did x which he thought the best thing to do.

Once again (1) and (2) cannot explain the fact stated by (3) since they are equivalent to (3).

This objection then fails. To know a man's reasons is to have the answer to one question about his actions, but there remains another which can only be answered by a scientific explanation.

There is, however, a further objection. This is that reason-giving and scientific explanations cannot supplement one another since they can never apply to the same thing. Scientific explanation is appropriate to events but not to actions, and vice versa. Now, on the one hand, the arguments above suggest that there *are* questions about actions which require a scientific explanation for their answer. On the other hand, there seems no reason to believe that actions and events are distinct types of occurrence. On the contrary actions appear to be simply events which we treat in a special way. We take an interest in the attitudes, motives and intentions of people whose behaviour plays a part in their occurrence. Now if to call an event an action is to express this kind of interest in it, and to imply such an interest to be appropriate, it will feel odd both to call something an action and to ask for a scientific explanation of it. But the fact that to call an event an action is to express one kind of interest in it, does not imply that it is to rule out all other kinds of interest.

Reasons may nevertheless seem specially appropriate to the explanation of human behaviour; they may interest us more than scientific explanations. Indeed it is sometimes claimed that science can in no way contribute to our understanding of human behaviour. Now reason-giving explanations provide the means of assessing both agents and actions and they help us to see consistency in behaviour when it is not apparent. If this is how we define 'understanding human behaviour', then knowing a man's reasons facilitates understanding and scientific explanation does not. But we do not have to define 'understanding' in this way. To do so is simply to express in another way the special interest we feel in reason-giving explanations.

A rather different view of the relationship between reasons and scientific explanation is that scientific explanations of human behaviour may be improved by taking into account the attitudes and beliefs constituting the reasons for the behaviour. This view of some psychologists and sociologists appears to result from their failure to distinguish a statement giving a reason from a causal hypothesis. They have noticed that 'A did x because of y' may be a correct explanation of x although y was not the case, so long as A thought it was, and have inferred that behaviour is correlated more closely with beliefs and attitudes than with actual situations. As a result they are inclined to argue that it is not a person's physical environment but his interpretation of it which determines his behaviour, and to advocate explanation in terms of beliefs, attitudes and perceptions. The best explanation of why a man made a detour on the road, they might say, is not that there was a hole in it, but that he believed there was.

But the consequence of replacing physical and social determinants by mental determinants in explanations of human behaviour would in fact be quite different from the one intended. Instead of a simple change of independent variables the result would change in the *type of explanation* from scientific explanation to either reason-giving, or what-explanation. The statement, "He made a detour because he believed there was a hole in the road", where it relates what a man said, is not typically a scientific or causal explanation. It reports a piece of reasoning, viz. "I thought that it was best to detour because of the hole in the road"; hence it may be a correct explanation although there was no hole. On the other hand, if the statement represents a hypothesis about a man's reasons or beliefs, it constitutes a what-explanation (see Chapters 4 and 5).

REASONS IN SOCIAL SCIENCE

Reasons cannot appear as variables in scientific explanations of human behaviour. However both reports of reasons and hypotheses concerning reasons figure in explanations in the social sciences. Evans-Pritchard's *Nuer Religion* is an example of the first. By reporting the Nuer's own reasons for their actions and beliefs he shows what might at first seem bizarre, or irrational, to be in fact natural and rational given their other beliefs and attitudes. In this way his reports enable us to understand Nuer behaviour *in the sense appropriate to this type of explanation, i.e. they enable us to assess it.* Further, if the Nuer act in accordance with fairly permanent attitudes and beliefs the reports will enable us to perceive their behaviour as falling into patterns. In so far as their behaviour is explained, however, it is explained by the Nuer themselves.

The situation is quite different when we attempt to explain the behaviour of other people by *hypotheses* about their attitudes and beliefs based upon observed regularities and patterns in their behaviour. In this case *we* provide the explanations, but they are not reason-giving explanations.

If they are to be useful in social science, hypotheses about attitudes and beliefs must be testable. This means that they must be sufficiently specific about the behaviour to be expected from someone having such an attitude or belief for it to be possible to deduce from them what he will do in a given situation. They must be in effect hypotheses about propensities to particular patterns of behaviour. An explanation employing such an hypothesis would have the following form:

(1) A has attitude x (where to have x is by definition to behave in a certain way e.g. to do things of type x in situations of type y);

(2) A is in a situation of type y;

(3) A does x.

This type of explanation (I shall label it behavioural explanation) shows why A does x by exhibiting his action as a part of a larger pattern of behaviour. It is a what-explanation.

Behavioural and reason-giving explanations are quite different. The expressions of attitude in reason-giving explanations are not empirical hypotheses about behaviour. Instead they report or express the beliefs and evaluative views a man holds or held. Thus although a reason-giving explanation may entail that a man thought a particular action good, or right, or best, it will not entail that he acted in a particular way, or indeed that he did anything at all. A man may take flowers to his wife if he wants to please her. But he may believe that diamonds or chocolates would please her just as much. In this case a reason-giving explanation is available whichever action he choses. Hence no such explanation entails one of these actions or excludes the others. Even if he had believed that flowers would please her most he need not have taken them, for a man may fail to do what he thinks best.

Although behavioural and reason-giving explanations are quite different they may easily be confused. "A did x because he wanted y", could be a report of a man's reasons, but it could also express a hypothesis. If explanations in terms of attitudes and motives are to be used in social science, care must be taken to distinguish in which sense they are intended.

The explanation of human behaviour in all its complexity by hypotheses about attitudes and beliefs presents problems. Consider the difficulty of calculating a man's wants, attitudes and beliefs from his behaviour. Given the behaviour one might, if one knew his attitudes and wants, guess his beliefs, and vice versa. But if neither is known, the possible combinations of beliefs and attitudes with which the behaviour would be consistent are infinite. Freud's writings, for example, show how almost any behaviour may be explained by sexual motives if suitable additional hypotheses are made about beliefs and the symbolic meaning of acts and objects.

The position is not improved by advancing a global hypothesis, as for example, "A man always acts from the strongest motive, or in such a way as to maximize the satisfaction of his various wants given the probable consequences of alternative actions". Such an hypothesis provides no way of predicting or explaining a man's behaviour unless the relative strength of his wants and the probability he attaches to the various possible outcomes of alternative actions are known.

A less ambitious project is to construct models of behaviour in narrow fields of activity e.g. a model of economic man, political man, sexual man, or logical man. Economic man might be defined as one who acts from the single motive of maximising utility, logical man as acting from the single desire to deduce. Such a model may be normative, setting out methods for making the correct or the best decisions in relation to a particular goal. In this case it could serve as a *guide* to decision making. On the other hand it may be descriptive, based upon observed patterns of behaviour. In either case we may hypothesise that a person's behaviour conforms to the model and then use it to explain his actions. In common with other explanations in terms of propensities or patterns of behaviour these will be what-explanations.

There seems to be no conflict between explanations in terms of models and reason-giving explanations. Normative models (e.g. the rules of deductive logic, the principles of classical economics) simply educate us in reasoning. A descriptive model provides us with information about how we have been behaving. Confronted by such information a person might say e.g. "It seems I always infer p from 'p implies q', and q. I know it's invalid, but that's the way I am", thereby abandoning rationality in this area. But he might say "My God how ridiculous I'll watch out in future". Which of these reactions occurs we must wait upon the development of models to discover.

CHAPTER 7

EXPLANATION IN HISTORY

SCIENTIFIC explanations involve universal propositions: events are explained by deducing their occurrence from universal propositions and statements about initial conditions. If a scientific explanation is correct the event explained had to happen, that is, the explanation does not leave open the possibility that the event might not have occurred. Finally, the correctness of the explanation is testable (though not provable) by making further deductions in other similar cases.

If you think of a historical event and try to imagine explaining it in a way which fulfils these criteria you will see the difficulties at once. The problem is to find a universal proposition which both fits the case to be explained and is not falsified by other cases. Consider the following example. Why did Henry VIII dissolve the monasteries? Because he needed money to finance his administration. What universal generalisation could one take to be implicit in this explanation? The most natural would be:

(1) whenever a king is in need of money to finance his administration he seizes monasteries.

This is plainly false. However, in a way it fails to capture the sense of the explanation and this might be better achieved by the following generalisation:

(2) whenever the supreme political authority needs finance it seizes that property the seizure of which is least likely to arouse either strong retaliation by the owners or widespread popular revolt.

But it seems likely that this also is false, for there must

have been occasions on which political authorities have needed finance and yet have not seized property. Moreover, the proposition is now so vaguely expressed that it would be difficult to test. How does one determine what action is least likely to produce a particular response? What measure of need is required?

(2) represents an attempt to improve upon (1) by making the generalisation wider in scope, i.e. by removing those restrictions on generality which appear to be peculiar to the case in question but not crucial to the general principle which seems to be involved. References to land and king are replaced by references to property and political authority, and the reference to particular sorts of property by a wider reference to the property seizure of which is likely to produce a substantial reaction. The advantage of these changes is that, for example, whereas (1) would be falsified in the case of a king who seized money but not land, (2) would not. Hence more types of situation are consistent with generalisation (2) than (1). On the other hand, since (2) is wider in scope than (1), the risk of finding counter-examples has also increased, for the generalisation now applies to all political authorities.

A second way of trying to improve upon (1) is by narrowing the scope of the generalisation to the point where it seems no counter-instances can be found. But this leads inevitably to a generalisation so narrow that it applies only to the case being explained:

(3) when a king exactly like Henry VIII in exactly the same situation, etc.

A proposition like (3) cannot be tested by application to other situations, hence it makes no sense to speak of confirming the explanation of which it is a part. Indeed if the phrase "in the same situation" involves being the ruler of England between the years 1509 and 1547, then (3) is no longer a generalisation at all since it applies to only one case.

It is sometimes claimed on behalf of historians that, although they cannot give deductive explanations of events, they *can* pick out the most important factors influencing, or leading to, the occurrence of a particular event. Thus David Ogg points to Mazarin's speculations with *rentes* as one of the main causes of the First Fronde, and modern historians assert that the entry of the United States into the Second World War was a major factor in the defeat of Hitler.

Most people would agree that the size of armies affects the outcome of a war, as does the relative extent of the combatants' economic resources. Similarly they would probably agree that widespread economic grievances are sometimes followed by civil disturbances. However the question at issue is whether one can assert of a *particular* event that certain particular factors were important in producing it.

A good analogy here is the explanation of a person's succumbing to a disease. If Smith died of tuberculosis we might well say that an important factor was the hypodermic injection of T.B. bacilli into his bloodstream. It is certainly true that the invasion of the body by T.B. bacilli is in general related to the manifestation of this disease. But what about Smith? It is not a general truth that whenever T.B. bacilli invade the body death ensues; it was therefore possible for Smith to survive the injections. He might, for example, have been previously vaccinated against T.B.; he might have had a high natural resistance; he might have had better medical treatment. One cannot say that the injection of bacilli was an important factor in Smith's death unless one has a way of measuring the importance of the injection in relation, let us say, to the absence of immunisation, Smith's level of natural resistance and the degree of competence of his doctors. All one can say is that the invasion of his body by the bacillus was a necessary condition of his dying of T.B. In other words the injection of bacilli was one of a class of events (the class: entries of this bacillus into a body) which is a necessary condition of the disease. This still, however, leaves open the possibility that the injection was in fact ineffective and that bacilli from another source caused the illness.

Returning to the American entry into the war against Hitler it is difficult to see how one appraises the importance of this event in relation, e.g. to the failure of German scientists to devise an atomic bomb or effective radar, or to the development of a resistance movement in occupied Europe. To make such assessments one has to be able to say such things as: even if Hitler had had an atomic bomb, the balance of power was in the allies' favour; even if Hitler had had the co-operation of the citizens in occupied territories, he would not have been victorious. But these statements imply that one could have measured the balance of forces and from this predicted with certainty the outcome of the war. In other words the ability to pick out certain events as important implies the ability to make predictions of a deductive kind; if one cannot do the latter one cannot legitimately do the former.

Looking back at events puts one in a rather special position. To use another analogy, we might say that an important factor in Jones's death was the arrival in his neighbourhood of a man-eating tiger. Of course from a knowledge of the tiger's arrival one could not easily predict

Jones's death. However, if we now know that the tiger ate Jones, then we can certainly attribute importance to the tiger's presence. Indeed if the tiger ate Jones then it is trivially true that the tiger played an important role in Jones's death. Similarly, if the Americans killed large numbers of German troops and occupied Germany, then it is trivially true that they played an important role in the defeat of Germany. If A defeats B then it is obvious that A's fighting B is an important factor in B's defeat, for "A defeated B" entails "A was fighting B". Further "A was fighting B" entails "A engaged in a fight with B". If then, knowing that A defeated B, we ask why B was defeated, it is easy to reply that an important factor was A's engaging in a fight with him, for this is entailed by what we know. In this case knowing that one event is an important factor in the occurrence of another is simply knowing that the two events occurred and, further, knowing some fact about the second event which by *itself* logically implies the occurrence of the first event. Such knowledge is not knowledge of a scientific or empirical kind. It involves no theories or laws about the relationship of events in the world, merely knowledge of various facts together with such trivial truths as "If a tiger eats a man it must be in the same place as the man", "If one army defeats another it must have engaged the other in battle".

There are further problems raised by the notion that historians are able to pick out the important factors in, or main causes of, events. Many seemingly scientific explanations of a causal nature are in fact not *simply* scientific. Suppose a hayrick burned down after a lighted cigarette stub had been dropped in it. We would say that the stub caused the fire. Why do we pick out the stub for special mention as *the* cause of the fire? Because, it may be suggested, it is the factor in the situation which can be controlled. But of course, even though it would be ridiculous to suggest this, the fire might have been prevented by the removal of the rick or by its isolation from oxygen. In other words other factors in the situation are equally subject to control. The truth seems to be that it is views about what is desirable and what is not desirable which determine which particular factor we choose as the cause. The existence of hayricks in free oxygen is desirable, but the dropping of cigarette stubs is not particularly desirable. We pick on the stub as the cause because the elimination of stub-dropping will be no loss to us. To select in this way from amongst those factors which would appear in a full account of the causation of an event is to evaluate the various factors contributing to the event's occurrence and to decide which it is desirable to eliminate (in the case of causes of bad things) and which to encourage (in the case of causes of good things).

The full scientific explanation of the burning hayrick is known in the sense that one knows which factors were relevant. In this case then evaluation is limited to appraising the result and deciding which factor to blame. In the case of human actions, for example a riot, or a murder, or in the case of political events, a declaration of war, the fall of a government, or the failure of a policy, we have so little idea of what a scientific account would be like that we may be evaluating already in selecting the factors which we regard as relevant. In investigating the causes of a war, should we examine the utterances of politicians, conflicts of economic or political interest, general attitudes in the community, educational systems, or the momentary dispositions of armies? No theory of political events exists to enable us to fit these various factors together in a complete explanation. If we could, however, arrive at a complete explanation of the situation, it would make no sense from the *scientific* point of view to pick out one or another of the factors in it as *the* cause, any more than it would make sense to decide that the presence of oxygen, the combustibility of the hay, or the presence of a cigarette stub, was most important in causing the fire. To pick out a particular factor as the cause, or main cause, of some event must always be to evaluate the situation by assigning responsibility and, hence, either praise or blame.

It is sometimes said that although there are no *universal* generalisations which historians can employ in the explanation of particular events, they may hypothesise connections between events over a certain historical period. Thus, although it is doubtful whether the introduction of free-trade always leads to an expansion of industry, a historian could supposedly hypothesise that between 1860 and 1914 freedom of trade led to an expansion of British industry. There are conditions under which such a claim is reasonable —for example, if the historian is prepared both to affirm a universal generalisation connecting free-trade in circumstances *c* with expansion of industry and to establish the fact that circumstances of type *c* obtained between 1860 and 1914. In the absence of these conditions hypotheses about relationships holding within certain periods of time are open to objection. All the coins in my pocket over a certain time may have been copper, but for me to claim, because of this, that they were copper because they were in my pocket would be absurd unless I were prepared to argue that any coin put in my pocket during that time would have become a copper coin. Such a claim could certainly be refuted, but it would make sense of my hypothesis that the coins in my pocket were copper *because* they were in my pocket. In the absence of such a claim all I am able to say is that the coins were in my pocket and that they were all copper. Similarly, a historian who is not prepared to generalise from the period 1860 to 1914 is not in a position to do more than point out two facts about the period: that it was a period of free-trade, and that it was a period of expansion of industry. He cannot claim a connection between the facts without committing himself to some form of generalisation.

Historical events are simply events in the past and they are as open to scientific explanation as any other events. However, scientific explanation requires that one show why an event happened in such a way as to exclude the possibility of any different outcome in the circumstances. It seems clear that at present few historical explanations can be regarded even as attempts at scientific explanation. If they are explanations which claim to show, as scientific explanations do, how one situation gives rise to, causes, or is a factor in the production of the other, but without recourse to the universal generalisations necessary to this type of explanation, then they must fail. On the other hand no plausible generalisation seems ever to be available to relate the events which historians regard as connected.

It is possible that some historians, in believing their explanations to be like scientific explanations, assume that there are true universal generalisations which justify their statements about the connections between events, although they cannot formulate them precisely. However the question whether or not one is explaining correctly is no different from the question whether or not the universal generalisations involved in one's explanation are true. If one is unable to identify these generalisations, one is unable to test them, and argument about the correctness of explanations cannot be systematic. The whole activity becomes one of undisciplined speculation. The apparent capacity of historical writing to explain is therefore illusory unless, perhaps, we are to regard such writing as offering explanations of some other non-scientific kind.

REASON-GIVING AND WHAT-EXPLANATIONS OF HUMAN ACTIONS IN THE PAST

Part of historical explanation consists in showing what sorts of reasons people could have had for doing what they did and then attributing one or another of these reasons to them. When a person has not expressed any reason for an action it is not a straightforward matter even to talk about *his reason*, since "his reason" always means, "the reason he gave or gives". One can avoid the difficulty by asking not about *his reason* but about *the reason why* he did what he did. Alternatively, it is permissible to hypothesise the reason he might have given had he been asked and had he answered candidly. To hypothesise in this way about a person's reasons involves speculating about his character, his likes, interests, and motives, and the principles he held on various issues.

Investigating what reasons a man might have had for doing something always involves two kinds of research. A fact is a reason if it is related to a particular action by some principle (moral or aesthetic), some obligation, or some desire or interest. To hypothesise, then, the reason a man might have had for doing something, is to hypothesise both about the facts and about his principles, feelings of obligation, desires, or interests. Facts may be difficult to check, particularly when they concern what a man hoped for or expected as a result of his action, but, except where some such mental state is involved, the sense in which they can be established is comparatively clear. This is not, however, true of hypotheses about a man's principles, feelings of obligation, motives, desires and interests. The indeterminacy of such hypotheses was pointed out in our discussion of explanation in terms of mental concepts.

Now, hypothesising about the reasons a man might have given for what he did is a peculiar activity if one's aim is to devise justifications and defences for his actions which the man himself might have pleaded. Such assessments and evaluations of actions and of character are important in everyday life, for they are related to actions we might take and attitudes we might form. But there are no actions to be taken with respect to figures of the past. On the other hand if one's hypothesising is aimed at relating facts about the period to the actions of individuals by means of suggested principles, intentions, motives and desires, the whole activity becomes one of explaining historical behaviour in terms of mental states. Such explanations, it was argued earlier, are what-explanations.

This type of explanation (what-explanations in terms of mental states) can be justified in ordinary life, but in the context of history it becomes much less clearly justifiable. When we explain behaviour by relating it to a state of mind, explaining kissing by love, crying by sorrow, conscientious objection by pacifist principles, we are fitting a particular piece of behaviour into one common pattern and excluding it from others. The fact that our hypothesis about the pattern may always be wrong, or at least may always be disputed, does not matter, for its value lies in enabling us to formulate an opinion about the future course of events and thus to adjust our behaviour to the behaviour of those we are trying to understand. Explanations of this kind cannot have this function or value when they are applied to figures and actions in history. Then they have all the uncertainty and difference of opinion associated with judgements about patterns in behaviour but lack the justification which there is for forming such hypotheses in everyday life that some hypothesis *must* be formed since some action must be decided upon. Moreover in the case of behaviour observed in the present we have two ways of testing any hypothesis. We can do so by continuing our observations over a period, or by adjusting our behaviour towards the person whose behaviour interests us and observing the consequences. The latter procedure is rather like the experimental investigation of an hypothesis, but it is not available as a means of testing hypotheses about historical figures. The problems here are analogous to those involved in the explanation of the behaviour of fictional characters, and a more detailed discussion of them is postponed to the chapter on explanation in literature. There is, however, one problem which is specially relevant here. Just as knowledge of a man's reasons, or his lack of them, justifies assessment of him as intelligent or stupid, logical or illogical, sophisticated or naive, etc., so, conversely, a choice between hypothetical explanations of his behaviour must depend upon an assessment of his intelligence, logicality, sophistication, etc. It is hard enough for an historian to defend his interpretation of a man's behaviour as reflecting certain attitudes and beliefs. But the difficulty is doubled if his interpretations must presuppose value judgements, for these must always be disputable.

NARRATIVE EXPLANATION

Much of history consists in telling us what happened and in what order. The ways in which such narrative history may be explanatory is illustrated by the following example. Smith asks Jones whether he can explain to him how Brown got to America. Jones replies that he came by ship, and, when Smith objects that Brown had no money, he replies that he travelled as a stowaway. The same explanation could have been given in straightforward narrative form. Brown was in England in 19—. He had no money but he managed to stow away on a ship leaving for America.

Smith's puzzlement, his need for an explanation, may take various forms. He may simply be unclear about the sequence of events. What he requires in this case is a clear statement of the manner in which Brown got to America. As one might ask how to make a souffle, so one might ask, after a souffle had been made, for an explanation of how it was made; as one might ask how to get from London to Birmingham, so one might ask, after someone had made the journey, for an explanation of how he did it. In these cases the question how something happened is a request for facts filling out the details and indicating what was done and what was not. The appropriate answer is a what-explanation of a very elementary kind. Let us call such explanation 'explanations of the manner in which something happened'.

On the other hand, Smith may be puzzled about how Brown was able to make the journey without money; he requires an explanation showing how it was possible. Let us call *these* explanations 'explanations of how something was possible'.

Explanations of the Manner in which Something Occurred. There are cases in which to seek an explanation of how something happened or was done is simply to seek knowledge of the manner in which it happened, or the means or method by which it was done. "How did the explosion occur?", "How did the government come to fall?" are questions which may be asked with this intent. A narrative may well show how something happened in this sense. The narrative of Brown's journey shows how he got to America in the sense that it describes his mode of travel. But Jones's account of how Brown got to America is not at all like the following explanation of how a bullet hit a vice-president: a rifle was fired at the president from a distance of 300 yards and the bullet left the muzzle with a velocity of x yards per second; the bullet, however, was deflected three feet by a forty m.p.h. cross-wind so that it struck the vice-president who was standing beside the president. This narrative contains information of such a kind and of such detail that it could be reformulated as an explanation of why the bullet had to hit the vice-president. We could not do this with the account of how Brown got to America, for there are no laws which apply there to compare with the laws of mechanics in the bullet example.

Explanations of how Something was Possible. It has recently been argued by W. H. Dray that historians explain events not by showing how, given certain facts and laws, the events had to occur, but by showing how it was *possible* for them to occur. He takes as an example the case of a baseball player who caught a ball thirty feet above the ground. Here is an event which puzzles us. We ask how it could have happened. Our problem is not to discover why it had to happen but what made it possible; discovering this removes our puzzlement and hence explains. The answer in this case is that the player ran up a ladder on the edge of the field and caught the ball as he reached the top.

What Dray fails to see, however, is that our notion of what is possible is simply the converse of our notion of what is impossible. We would have regarded the catch as impossible because of various assumptions and beliefs about the human anatomy, about the geography of the field, and about the laws of physiology and mechanics. Given that these were correct, it would be possible to predict in a scientific way that the catch would not occur. But the assumptions were wrong; there was a ladder. In other words, showing how an event is possible consists simply in showing that a proof of impossibility is based on wrong assumptions. If we did not have at the back of our minds scientific theories and assumptions about facts in the light of which a particular event appeared impossible, we would have nothing against which to oppose the view that the event was possible. Such a scientific account shows us *on what grounds* the event might be thought impossible. It also indicates what changes must be made in our assumptions if we are to conceive it possible.

Since statements about possibility are the contradictories of statements about impossibility, one cannot have the one without the other. It makes no sense to speak of historians showing how something was possible if one cannot speak of them showing how something was impossible. But to show that an event was impossible is to deduce from theories and facts that it did not occur, and this implies the practicability of scientific explanation.

One may show *that* something was possible in two ways:

(1) by showing that the relevant laws and the known facts do not rule it out;

(2) by showing that it happened.

To show *how* something was possible is to show that there are laws and facts which explain it; or to show that, although the laws and facts appear to rule it out, the assumed facts are false, while the laws along with the new facts explain or might explain it. Showing how something was possible involves a full-blown scientific account of its occurrence. Consequently a narrative only shows how something was possible if the facts it presents are covered by theories capable of providing such an account, or if it is itself an elliptical version of such an account.

However it is possible for a narrative to *appear* to show how something was possible though in fact, it does not. People come to the events of the past, as to those of the present, with beliefs about what is and what is not possible. Such beliefs can be formulated as general propositions about necessary conditions.

Examples of such beliefs are the following:
- One cannot make a cake without eggs.
- One cannot make a dress with less than three yards of material.
- One cannot become president within the term of office of a president unless he dies.
- One cannot break a wall twenty feet thick without the use of gun-powder.
- One cannot get from Moscow to London in four hours.
- One cannot run a government without finance.

An event which appears to conflict with such beliefs may give rise to puzzlement. For example, Smith's belief that one cannot cross the Atlantic without money made him puzzled when he learnt that Brown had arrived in America. A narrative may dispel such puzzlement by presenting facts which show the event to be consistent with our beliefs (in Smith's case, for example, by revealing that Brown did have money) or by causing us to revise our general beliefs (in Smith's case, by causing him to realise that stowaways can cross the Atlantic *without* money). Such narratives are similar to those which really show how something was possible in as much as the puzzlement they remove arises out of an apparent inconsistency between general beliefs and the facts as known. The difference, and it is an important one, is that here the general beliefs are not true. For this reason, although the reader's puzzlement is removed, and he thinks he sees how something was possible, he is mistaken. One only sees how something was possible when one can relate it to general beliefs which are true (or at least well-confirmed). If I believe that witchcraft only works within five miles of a witch, I may be puzzled at reports of the death by witchcraft of a man at some greater distance. On learning that he was in fact within a five-mile radius of the witch, my puzzlement is removed; I think I see how it was possible for him to be struck down by the spells. But I am mistaken, for the question how he died, or how it was possible for him to die, cannot be answered by reference to witchcraft, beliefs about the effectiveness of witchcraft being as they are false.

One should, possibly, regard narrative history as pre-emptive, providing facts which lie in wait to allay the puzzlement to which our beliefs predispose us. But if this is its function it is a quite different one from that of providing accounts which really show how things are possible.

JUDGEMENT IN HISTORY

There is yet another kind of activity, common in ordinary life, which might be held to resemble what the historian does when he explains. We often feel, though unable to predict with accuracy the future course of political or economic events, or the development of personal relationships, quite able to set out the possibilities, allowing some and excluding others. Thus a political commentator might well claim that, although he could never precisely predict future events, he could always select a set of possibilities one of which would be correct. This ability is what we would call political judgement, and comparable to it is our ability to assess the likelihood of this or that behaviour in our friends, or the tipster's ability to name the likely winners. One might regard a historian as a man of judgement in this sense, capable of looking at a past situation and judging its probable outcome. One could then regard the historical explanation of a past event as an attempt so to present the facts of a situation that the event to be explained seems one of the most likely upshots.

Judgement of this kind is a *skill*; it is not a *method* and this has important consequences. One may test a particular man's skill in predicting the outcome of events or situations by seeing how often and within what limits he is successful. Moreover, the possession of such skills must be regarded as valuable. But they are personal skills. Each man's ability to judge the likely course of events has to be tested. By contrast, a *method* of predicting involves rules by which predictions are made. If such rules are tested and found capable of guiding predictions successfully, then they may be used by anyone. Where personal skills are involved one can only estimate the satisfactoriness of particular judgements by testing the skill of the judger. Returning to history, one can see that, if writing history is the exercise of judgement, then the writings of a particular historian can only be assessed by testing his skill in judgement. In other words, one cannot assess historians' judgements without subjecting them to tests of their ability to predict (without prior knowledge) the outcomes of past situations. But, since it is unlikely that a historian would have no prior knowledge of the very events that he is studying, this kind of test is ruled out.

More important, while skills in judgement are valuable from a practical point of view, they are theoretically value-less. While one would respect a farmer who was able to judge with considerable accuracy the outcome of an experiment in cross-breeding, one would value far more a theory which enabled anyone to breed in a predictable way. It is not just that the farmer's knowledge (skill) is personal and dies with him. There are other advantages in being able to express knowledge in hypotheses besides that of easy dissemination. When one attempts to express knowledge in the form of hypotheses and theories one opens the doors to systematic research, to the possibility of discovering why one particular prediction was right and another wrong.

There are many reasons why we think it of value to study history. One may be that doing so develops and improves our judgement. Nevertheless, the skill of judgement is different from the ability to explain. A man may be good at picking the winners but quite unable to explain why a given horse won.

CHAPTER 8

ASPECTS OF EXPLANATION IN LITERATURE AND CRITICISM

In literary criticism one finds, amongst others, explanations of evaluative judgements, explanations of meaning, explanations of what a work is or is about, its main point or essential characteristic, and explanations of the behaviour of characters. Within literature itself one finds explanations of particular actions and of the behaviour of particular people. Explanations in criticism and in literature give rise to rather different problems, the former to the problems of interpretation (both of meaning and of behaviour) and justification (of critical judgements), the latter to the problems of literary truth and plausibility. I shall discuss explanations in criticism first, beginning with explanations of critical value judgements and then turning to explanations of the behaviour of fictional characters. The problems of explaining meaning are treated in the second part of the book.

EXPLANATIONS OF CRITICAL VALUE JUDGEMENTS

Our aesthetic beliefs and judgements are as open to scientific explanation as our other beliefs and actions; this is the concern of psychologists. The philosophical problems associated with such explanations are a part of the philosophy of science; they are not specifically problems of criticism. However, we also explain our aesthetic value judgements by giving reasons and these explanations are of special interest to us here since a large part of the philosophy of criticism concerns the justification of evaluative critical judgements.

I argued in Chapter 6 that someone explains his beliefs, when he gives his reasons for holding them, by making clear why he thinks them correct or true. This holds equally of value beliefs and judgements. To explain why one believes a novel or picture good (by giving reasons) is to show why one thinks these beliefs to be correct or right.

A man may claim that an aesthetic value judgement is correct on various grounds. For example he may cite what he takes to be expert opinion, or refer to a writer's other works as evidence of his skill. But where, e.g. a novel or poem is available to him and it is his own critical judgement he wishes to defend he must do so by reference to features of the work itself which satisfy his own criteria of excellence.

To refer to any property p as a reason for judging a work of art good is to imply that one holds as a principle that any similar work possessing this property is equally commendable.

Consequently when someone calls a novel a good novel because it has p, he is committed to the principle that any p novel is good. Should we discover another novel which this man concedes to have p, yet refuses to judge as good, he stands convicted of inconsistency. He must either change his assessment of one of the novels or revise his reason for commending the first thereby revising also his aesthetic principles. There is an analogy here with the way in which scientific explanations imply universal generalisations, and with the testing of such generalisations. But it is only an analogy, for evaluative principles are not empirical hypotheses and the issue in the present case is whether a man's explanations are consistent, not whether they are correct. We can deduce from the principle implied in a man's explanation of a critical judgement what his evaluation of another work should be. But the principle is not falsified if his evaluation differs from the one predicted. This merely shows him to be committed to a second principle inconsistent with the first. This result is nevertheless important for it forces him to revise and clarify his aesthetic views.

To list properties of works of art, or reactions to them, which count as reasons for judging them good would be simply to express one's own aesthetic opinions. However, it is possible, without begging evaluative questions, to classify properties and reactions which are referred to in giving reasons. Such a classification might be the following.

(1) *Factual Properties.* For example, the subject matter of a novel or picture, its structure, the characters and their relationships, aspects of language and style in writing, arrangments of colours and shapes in pictures. (Properties in this class will of course often be the subject of interpretative disputes.)

(2) *Success Properties.* These imply a particular kind of excellence, e.g., well structured, convincing, realistic, accurate, imaginative, elegant, balanced.

(3) *Appropriate Response Properties.* These imply that a particular response is appropriate, e.g. interesting, exciting, moving, stimulating, enjoyable, pleasant, exhilarating.

(4) *Personal Reactions.* I enjoyed it, I liked it, I found it interesting, I was moved by it, etc.

Now if p is a success or appropriate response property, to assert a work to be p will itself be to evaluate it as possessing a particular merit or demerit, or as warranting a particular response. Such an evaluation will in turn require an explanation, or justification, in terms of further properties q, presumably from category (1), and further principles. But to ascribe a success or appropriate response property is to assess only one aspect of a work; a novel may be bad though interesting, or well written. Consequently the principles implied here will be of restricted scope, e.g. that one should be moved by a novel which is q, or that the test of stylistic excellence, is q.

A personal response (category (4)) is sometimes cited in defence of a critical opinion; asked why he thinks a novel good a man may reply that he enjoyed reading it, or was moved by it. Now he might wish to imply that his enjoyment of it is a sufficient reason for thinking the novel good, though if he could not say what he enjoyed about it, or why he thought this reaction appropriate, his remark, besides appearing egotistical, might seem more concerned with himself than the novel. However the normal implication would be rather that he thought the novel enjoyable, and on *that* ground judged it good. But the fact that he enjoyed reading it is not merely a poor reason for calling a novel good, it is a poor reason for regarding it as enjoyable, since it does not show why this response was appropriate. Consequently his reply will normally carry the further implication that he believes the work to have characteristics, q, presumably from category (1) or (2), which would warrant the description of it as enjoyable.

Explanations of critical value judgements in terms of properties and facts in categories (2)–(4), then, imply further explanations in terms of properties in category (1). Now we often find it difficult to explain our reasons for an aesthetic judgement where these refer to factual properties. Yet despite our inability to state them, we feel we have reasons.

We believe that we detect something in the work, which if we could identify it more precisely, we would give as our reason for the judgement. Faced with this difficulty in describing the characteristic of the work which we believe would justify our view of it as e.g. disturbing, or imaginative, or simply good, we often attempt to indicate it by pointing. Someone might say, for example:

– It's this that makes it so good.
– Here is an example of what I mean by his elegance of style.
– It has something to do with the way he places these two shapes.
– Listen to this bit; this is what distinguishes him from his more mediocre contemporaries.

It might be argued that such remarks must point not to reasons but to causes, to features, the occurrence of which in a work tends to correlate with his commendation of it. Thus there might seem an inconsistency in holding that a man might believe a work to possess a particular property p, believe it good, or excellent in virtue of p, and therefore be committed to the principle that p works are good, yet be incapable of saying what p is. How *can* he subscribe to the view that p works are good if he cannot say what p is? If we were to interpret his statement as an attempt to indicate a characteristic correlated with his judgements about this and other similar works, there would be no problem.

Suppose that by an empirical investigation we were able to identify the properties of works of art correlated with a persons's aesthetic judgements; we could then say, "The paintings he calls good all have property p" (or "The buildings he thinks well proportioned all conform to the golden section"). Thus it might seem that if a man is unable to say exactly what he judges good in a work of art, an empirical investigation will identify it for him. Moreover it might be argued that a proper empirical investigation is a *better* method of determining the features of a work in virtue of which a man commends it than his own judgements as to his reasons, even when these are explicit.

These suggestions imply that a man who states or indicates what he thinks good in a work of art (and thinks by this means to justify his aesthetic judgement), is, in reality, trying to identify characteristics the presence of which correlates generally with his commendation of this and similar works. On this view the statement "I commend it because it has property p" is to be interpreted as an empirical hypothesis. Its function, therefore, cannot be to justify or defend an aesthetic judgement. Instead it might be to influence opinion, by directing attention to aspects of a work likely to elicit a particular response.

Let us examine more carefully the consequences of empirical investigations of value judgements. Suppose it is discovered that the novels I think good all possess a certain property, q. Now it may be that I commended them for this reason. Alternatively I may now realise for the first time that q is what distinguishes them as good. In either case I shall in future give q as my reason when I commend a novel. Moreover if in the past I judged a novel good in virtue of a property (whether I named it or merely indicated it) which I now believe to be identified as q, I shall claim that I am now able to explain more precisely my reasons for those earlier judgements.

However although as a result of such an investigation I may know that I always commend q novels, if I refuse to subscribe to the view that q novels are good, I shall *not* give q as a reason for future commendations. In response to the statement "Novels you judge good are all q", I shall reply, "True, but this is not what I think good about them".

Similarly if I do not think q identifies what I regarded as the virtue of these books I shall say, "It may be a fact that I always commended q novels, but it was not because of q".

Empirical investigations only show us what our reasons are (or were) if we agree that the properties correlated with our judgements are those in virtue of which we make (or made) them.

Knowing which properties of works of art are correlated with them certainly enables us to explain and predict a man's aesthetic judgements. But explanations in terms of correlations are not reason-giving but what-explanations. A man who explains his opinions in this way can claim no special authority. If he says, for example "I praise x because it is y", it is appropriate to reply, "You may be right, but it will be necessary to check whether in fact you praise things which are y". Moreover this explanation is not a comment on the work of art, x, putting forward a reason for praising it, it is a comment by the speaker on himself. Consequently if we were to disagree with him the issue would not be an evaluative one, whether y is a reason for praising x, but a factual one, whether the works he praises are in general y.

In fact there is no inconsistency in the idea that a man might have a reason which he cannot specify so long as (1) he is able to direct attention to some characteristic of a work; and (2) he would evaluate in the same way any similar work possessing this characteristic. He does subscribe to an evaluative principle although he is able to express it only by examples. We sometimes choose to express an opinion in this way when we could if we wished be more explicit. We might say e.g., explaining why we believe war to be wrong, "Look at these children who are its victims".

EXPLANATIONS OF THE BEHAVIOUR OF FICTIONAL CHARACTERS

I begin with some examples drawn from *Hamlet and the Philosophy of Criticism* by Morris Weitz. A. C. Bradley sets out to explain Hamlet's behaviour, in particular Hamlet's delay in avenging his father's death. He examines various theories or explanations: that there were external impediments—for example, the King being well guarded; that Hamlet desired the public punishment of the King so that the justice of the punishment would be apparent (this would have taken time to arrange); that there were features of Hamlet's beliefs and character which impeded his action— for example, that he had moral scruples about murder, or that he was over-intellectual in character, all thought and no action, or that he was in a state of deep melancholy. Bradley then rules out the first and second explanations on the ground of internal evidence in the play. The first is excluded since on at least one occasion Hamlet could have killed the King but did not. Similarly, he rules out moral scruples by pointing to passages in the play where Hamlet clearly acknowledges a duty to kill his father's assassin. Over-thoughtfulness he excludes on the ground that there is in general no reason to associate thoughtfulness with inaction (a supposed fact of psychology). And so we are left with deep melancholy. Bradley suggests that the re-marriage of Hamlet's mother is a shock which throws him into a deep melancholy and indeed, according to Bradley, Hamlet displays just that particular combination of qualities which defines melancholy: brooding, irritability, obsessiveness and callousness. The two essential factors in Bradley's explanation of Hamlet's behaviour are thus (1) a hypothesis about Hamlet's character; and (2) a hypothesis about the cause of a change in Hamlet's manifest character.

Hypotheses about the Character of Hamlet. Bradley states that the only way in which a conception of Hamlet's character could be proved true would be to show that this conception *alone* explains all of the relevant facts presented in the text. He is surely right in this, but he omits to draw the conclusion that no such proof or anything like it is possible. It has already been argued that explanations in terms of character or mental states are what-explanations: they tell us what is going on and fit the piece of behaviour which interests us into a larger pattern. Critical disputes about how to explain the behaviour of characters arise because different critics argue for different patterns. Resolution of such disputes, as Bradley sees, depends on proving one pattern to be the true one. Unfortunately proofs of this kind are not possible.

Given any set of data (for example, the text of *Hamlet*) it is always possible to hypothesise a variety of patterns. A simple geometric analogy will help make this point clear. What is the pattern in these five dots?

The following are all possible, and there are many others:

Critics make a variety of suggestions about the pattern in Hamlet's behaviour, that it was the behaviour of a melancholic, a mentally unstable person or an over-intellectual person, of a man pre-occupied with the problem of good and evil or with political ambition, of a neurotic with repressed incestuous feelings for his mother and fear of his father, or of a man stricken by grief. There is no more a way of deciding which is correct here than there is in the case of the five dots.

There are no facts which *have* to be seen as belonging to this pattern or that. Any fact can, with the help of suitable adjustments and subsidiary hypotheses, be fitted into any hypothesised pattern; and the same is true of any group of facts. You can perform an experiment to convince yourself of this. Think of someone whom you know fairly well and about whose character you have formed some opinion. Now imagine him doing something which forces you to revise your interpretation or estimation of his previous behaviour. You will find that enormous revisions are possible. Consider, too, how our estimates of the character and motives of politicians and historical figures change as new facts emerge, and how the old facts can always be re-interpreted to fit the new estimates.

It may be argued that although any particular set of bits of behaviour can be interpreted in different ways, nevertheless there is at least this difference between Hamlet and an historical figure like Gladstone: no new facts will ever be discovered about Hamlet. That particular stimulus to re-interpretation will never be presented to us. But this objection does not meet the original point, which was that any data about behaviour are open to a wide variety of interpretations or judgements as to the pattern they represent.

The suggestion above that new information can be a stimulus to re-interpretation was only intended to make this vivid. One does not *need* such a stimulus to think up alternative interpretations; one needs only imagination. However, the fact that no new data about Hamlet's behaviour will ever be discovered *is* important. It brings up a major contrast between explanations of behaviour in criticism and explanations of behaviour in ordinary life.

If I say that Fred loves his wife Mary, I am not simply describing his behaviour to date (saying what he did), I am fitting it into a pattern. Now suppose that tomorrow he murders Mary, apparently for her money; I may, though I need not, revise my view about the pattern in Fred's behaviour. I may say that my previous judgement that he loved Mary was wrong. That I am able to revise my views in the light of further information shows that my original statement about Fred's feeling for Mary was, though based on behaviour I had observed, concerned with more than that. It was a statement about a pattern in Fred's behaviour towards Mary, hence it was about *all* of that behaviour, past, present, and future. My statement was meant, in fact, to imply that Fred's behaviour had never been and would never be such as to lead me to revise my view of his feelings for Mary. It was suggested in an earlier chapter that this ordering of our expectations is the main function of mental-concept explanations.

It must be emphasised that *any* hypothesis about a pattern in someone's behaviour can be disputed by someone with an alternative hypothesis, and any new data which we consider force us to revise our views *may* be considered by someone else to be perfectly compatible with the view we hold. So that no such hypothesis is provable on any set of data and no facts can ever *compel* us to revise it. Such hypotheses cannot be proved right, and if we are determined to hold them we cannot be forced by logic or by fact to give them up. A woman who clings to the belief that her husband loves her, explaining away his embezzlement of her money and apparent attempts to kill her, may appear foolish or unwise but she is not in the light of the facts necessarily wrong. Men sometimes kill women they love and, perhaps more frequently, they defraud them of money.

We may devise test situations. For example, a business-man who has become doubtful of his partner's honesty may test him by putting opportunities for embezzlement in his way, or a wife, uncertain of her husband's loyalty, may contrive that a situation arises in which it is put to the test. Such tests, however, though they provide additional data, cannot be thought of as tests to determine the truth or falsity of a hypothesis. Rather they create new situations of practical importance. Suppose the husband in the example succumbs. Must his wife say that he is not loyal? Surely not. She might find ways of excusing his conduct. The test situation does not *force* her to decide that he either is or is not loyal, but it may make her decide that she will no longer treat him as loyal. She may revise her view as to how to behave towards him, and she may express this decision by saying, "He is not a loyal husband". Judgements of a person's motives and character go hand in hand with decisions about how to behave towards that person. They are of great practical importance since they guide our behaviour towards other people. They are the rationalis-ations of our choices and decisions with regard to others.

Of course judgements about the mental state or character of a person are not *simply* expressions of decisions about how

to behave towards that person. They are based on observation and whatever pattern one claims to see in the facts has
to accommodate the facts. If the behaviour observed were
very typical of a man in love it would be difficult to hold an
alternative view; to do so might, for example, involve
imagining quite complex motives on his part. The point is
that the decision to accept one hypothesis rather than
another is linked to alternative courses of action, and, if we
are strongly inclined to treat a person in a particular way,
we may well devise quite complex hypotheses to make our
judgement of that person consistent with our actions. We
will still, of course, have to make our complex hypotheses
plausible, to see that they both fit his behaviour to date and
allow for the behaviour we expect from him in the future.

Any judgement of the pattern in a person's behaviour,
then, will:

(1) since it can be often revised in the light of his unobserved and future behaviour, often involve expectations
about that unobserved and future behaviour (particularly in
the case of character-traits or long-term emotions);

(2) since it represents one's view of the way he behaves
and will behave (unless he changes), be influenced by and to
some extent represent inclinations to behave towards him
in this way or that;

(3) be testable by devising test situations. The test, however, will not eliminate the possibility of sticking to the
original judgement in a more complicated and elaborate
form. Thus accepting the result of a test as grounds for
revising a judgement represents a decision about how
complex a hypothesis one is prepared to bother with.

Explanation of the behaviour of fictional characters in
terms of mental states may be contrasted with scientific

explanation. But it may also be contrasted with the mental-concept explanations we make in ordinary life. Critical explanations of this type get the worst of all worlds. They are not related to what they explain by relationships of entailment, hence they cannot be demonstrated to be false. Moreover all the data are before us, so that no experiments can be performed to help us decide between rival hypotheses. The question whether Hamlet was melancholic or over-intellectual is like the question whether the group of dots

•   •

•

•   •

conforms to this pattern   or this

In giving critical explanations we seem to be stating the truth and that plainly is an illusion. Less obviously illusory is the sense that such explanations are as valid as those we give of behaviour in ordinary life. But this, too, is an illusion for, although in both cases judgements about pattern are necessarily problematical, in ordinary life we *can* perform further tests and, more important, we are governed in making our judgements by the necessity of living with the consequences of them.

EXPLANATIONS WITHIN LITERATURE

There is a passage in *Swann's Way* where Proust gives an explanation of how one may fall in love.

Among all the methods by which love is brought into being, among all the agents which disseminate that blessed bane, there are few so efficacious as the great gust of agitation which, now and then, sweeps over the human spirit. For then the creature in whose company we are seeking amusement at the moment, her lot is cast, her fate and ours decided, that is the creature whom we shall henceforward love. It is not necessary that she should have pleased us, up till then, any more, or even as much as others. All that is necessary is that our taste for her should become exclusive. And that condition is fulfilled so soon as—in the moment when she has failed to meet us—for the pleasure which we were on the point of enjoying in her charming company is abruptly substituted an anxious torturing desire, whose object is the creature herself, an irrational, absurd desire, which the laws of civilised society make it impossible to satisfy and difficult to assuage—the insensate, agonising desire to possess her.

Marcel Proust, *Swann's Way*
(trans. C. K. Scott Moncrieff)

At first it seems that Proust is offering a scientific, or covering law, explanation, complete with universal generalisation. But it is obviously not the case that every man who has a moderate interest in a woman will develop a passionate love for her if she fails to keep an appointment with him. Again, his explanation might be regarded as tautologous: a man who develops an exclusive taste for a woman has already fallen in love with her. Probably what Proust had in mind, however, was that this sort of thing *can* happen, mild interest and disappointment may be followed by a more passionate interest. There are people who react in this way and their behaviour is to be explained by saying that they are that kind of person; it is a possible way of behaving.

There is a fairly widespread view that one of the functions of novelists is to represent possible people and possible ways of behaving and in this way extend our knowledge of and sensitivity to people in real life. The idea, however, of a possible type of person, or a possible way of behaving, or a possible relationship, is quite a complex one. It is important first to distinguish between two sorts of possibility, *logical* and *actual* possibility. To say that something is *logically* possible is to say that it is not self-contradictory. A female brother is not possible logically, because it is a self-contradictory notion, as is the notion of a round square. Anything which is not self-contradictory is logically possible—for example, a man fifteen feet high, a marrow the size of a house, jumping to the moon. But many things that are logically possible could never really happen; they are not *actually* possible. What this means is that, if we accept certain propositions as true, then it follows by deductive logic that these things cannot occur. For example, if we see Jones on our right, it follows logically that we do not see him on our left; hence, if we believe that we see him on our right, we must think it impossible for him to be on our left. Now of course it is logically possible for Jones to be anywhere; when we say that it is not possible for him to be on our left, we mean only that *if we see him on our right*, then it is not possible for him to be on our left. The case of a man jumping to the moon is a clear one. Jumping to the moon is not logically impossible; it is not nonsense; it is imaginable. But, given the truth of the law of gravity and given the physiology of the human body, it obviously could not happen.

Saying that a thing *x* is actually impossible always implies a reference to some facts (or supposed facts) with which the occurrence of *x* would be inconsistent. The logically impossible is self-contradictory; the actually impossible is only inconsistent with beliefs which we take to be true. To say then that something is actually possible is to say that there is nothing in our beliefs about the world which rules it out.

Turning back to literature, it seems clear that, whereas some writers are interested in the exploration of what is logically possible within certain fairly narrow limits (an interest in fantasy), most novelists are concerned to portray actually possible people and ways of behaviour. If part of the value of a novel is held to be that it portrays actually possible people or behaviour or situations, then in evaluating a work we are called on to decide whether the people, situations, and behaviour portrayed *are* in fact actually possible. If we are unable to decide this, then we are unable to evaluate the work on these grounds. Now, there are only two ways of showing that people or behaviour as described in a novel are actually possible, one, by producing real people or behaviour, the other, by showing that the people or behaviour portrayed are consistent with the laws of psychology. Unfortunately the science of psychology has not yet reached the point where its laws are sufficiently universal in character and wide in scope to be of use in this connection. The only way, then, of determining whether a character or the behaviour of a character in a novel is actually possible is by appeal to similar people and behaviour in real life.

Of course people will speculate about the possibility of behaving in this or that way, about the plausibility of this or that description of a character's behaviour. But all such speculation *is* mere speculation. It is as though someone had written a book on minerals in the Middle Ages and its reader had speculated about whether it were possible for iron to do this, or gold that. Such speculation without a good theory of the chemistry of elements would have been fruitless. Experiment would have been the only profitable course to pursue. So it is with speculation about the events and characters in novels.

CHAPTER 9

MEANING: INTRODUCTION

MANY of the controversies which we engage in over the course of our lives seem to end in disputes about meaning. Arguments about matters of morality quickly lead to, and often become bogged down in, disputes about what it means to say that one *ought* to do something, or that something is *good*—for example, whether moral judgements are 'objective', or 'subjective', and so on. A similar fate tends to befall arguments in criticism. Frustrating as this may be, one must resist the temptation of thinking that questions about meanings are trivial, the real and important questions being the moral and aesthetic ones. In a sense, obviously, this is true, and, if all problems about meaning were just difficulties due to ambiguity, or to differences in the way different people use words, that *would* reduce questions about meaning to a fairly insignificant role. But this is not at all the situation. The problem with moral and aesthetic judgements (and one could add causal, inductive, mental, explanatory and existential judgements) is not that people are at cross-purposes when they make them, meaning different things by what they say; it is that, although the sentences used in making these judgements are clearly meaningful, although in a sense we must know what we mean by them since we use them, no one can say just what they do mean. Of course attempts are made but none prove entirely successful. Questions about meaning are crucial, then, in any consideration of moral, critical and explanatory arguments because they are involved in discovering just what sorts of judgements these arguments are about.

Questions of meaning arise more specifically in literary criticism, and in the criticism of other arts where the material to be examined and criticised has meaning. Part of a literary critic's task is to explain the meaning of literary works or give interpretations of them. These activities must raise general questions about meaning and interpretation. For example, in determining the meaning of a passage what role should the intention of the writer play, or the reaction of the reader, or can it be decided just by looking at the words? How does the metaphorical use of words differ from the standard use of words? Do words have different meanings for different people? In interpreting and criticising works of literature, and in looking at and commenting upon pictures, one makes judgements which to some extent presuppose answers to these questions about meaning: one assumes, without thinking, a certain answer to be correct. The nature of meaning is a difficult problem and the assumptions about it to which one is naturally prone are likely to be wrong.

CHAPTER 10

CAUSAL THEORIES OF MEANING

THERE seem to be two groups of questions about meaning. The first contains what-questions: What is meaning? What are meanings? What is it for two words to have the same meaning, or one word two meanings? The second contains how-questions: How do words mean? How do I know what words to use to convey what I mean? How do we understand the words that others utter? One striking and attractive characteristic of a causal theory of meaning is that it seems fitted to answer both types of question telling us not only what meaning is, but also how words acquire meaning and how communication occurs.

The notion basic to a causal theory is that words come to have meaning by a process like conditioning, as a consequence of which each of them produces when uttered a particular effect in the mind of the hearer. Experiments with dogs and other animals have shown how a response initially made to one situation (or stimulus) may be transferred to another by conditioning. A dog naturally salivates at the smell and sight of food. If each time he is given food a bell is rung just before he gets it, he will eventually come to salivate when the bell rings, even if the food does not arrive. There are a number of ways in which one could describe this phenomenon. One could say that what used to be a response to food has become a response to the bell, or that the bell has become a sign for food, or that the bell makes the dog expect or think of food. However, the important step in arguing a causal theory of meaning is to describe learning the meaning of words as a process not unlike the conditioning of the dog. I. A. Richards in *The Philosophy of Rhetoric* does this in the following way. Whenever, he says, one is engaged in learning the meaning of a word one is in a situation which has two major aspects: (1) a physical context (the objects and physical events in one's surroundings); and (2) a psychological context (the events in and states of one's own mind at that time). These two contexts are related, for the things one perceives will belong in the physical context, while one's perceptions of them will be part of the psychological context. One's perceptions of, and thoughts about, the physical context may be regarded as natural or unconditioned responses to that context, responses which can, however, come to be evoked by words as well as by their original stimuli. Teaching the meaning of a word consists in uttering the word in various contexts so that it becomes associated with one particular aspect or part of them. Thus, if the word "table" is uttered in contexts embracing a physical table and a perception of a table, it will come to be associated with tables and to produce the psychological response previously only produced by the tables themselves. Naturally, the theory does not suggest that the word will induce us to see tables when there are none there. Causal theorists tend in fact to be rather unspecific about the effect a word produces in the mind. However, the central idea is clear: every word we learn comes to produce a particular mental state, belief, thought, or image, of or about the corresponding thing in the physical world. Richards speaks of words as having "delegated efficacy", and he seems to mean that words take on some of the power to produce effects on the mind that objects normally have. The word "table" acquires some of the powers of tables, the word "love" some of the powers of love, etc.

This, in outline, is the way in which a causal theorist answers questions about how words get meaning. The extension of the account to explain how we understand one another is quite complicated but the main idea is this: one person's thought, or belief, is causally associated with certain words which, when uttered, cause another person to have the same, or similar, thoughts or beliefs.

In answering questions about what meanings are, or what the meaning of a particular word is, causal theories allow a certain freedom and consequently a certain variety. One might, as a causal theorist, choose to say, as Richards does in *The Philosophy of Rhetoric*, that the meanings of words are the objects and situations in the world for which the words have delegated efficacy; the meaning of "table" is this or that particular table. On the other hand one might choose to say that the meaning of a word is the *effect* it produces in the mind of a hearer. One version of this type of account appears in C. L. Stevenson's *The Language of Ethics*. For various reasons Stevenson modifies the account: the meaning of a word is not the effect it produces in a hearer's mind but rather its power or disposition to produce such effects, the meaning of a particular word being a function of the particular effects it is capable of producing.

In *The Meaning of Meaning* by Ogden and Richards there is the diagram shown opposite. The diagram is intended to show the complex relationship which the authors believe holds between objects and words when words have a meaning. Both object and word produce mental effects, and the effects they produce are similar, but the relationship between them is an indirect one: they are causally related to the same or similar mental states. From the diagram it is not clear whether

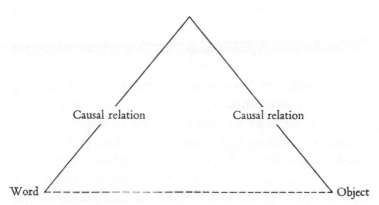

Thoughts and beliefs

Causal relation   Causal relation

Word   Object

we are to regard the thoughts and beliefs or the object as the meaning of the word. In fact, as we shall see later, causal theorists are inclined to speak of objects as meanings when they are interested in explaining how words are related to the world, and of ideas in the mind as meanings when their concern is with how we understand one another's speech.

We have noticed one attractive characteristic of causal theories of meaning, namely, that they appear to be capable of explaining both what meaning is and how words come to have it. There is another attraction. Causal theories can be extended and elaborated so as to suggest answers to some very complex questions about the nature of evaluative and metaphorical discourse.

Emotive Meaning. Stevenson's main purpose in adopting a causal theory of meaning appears to be to give legitimacy to a notion he wishes to introduce, the notion of 'emotive meaning'. Stevenson wants to explain the distinctive character of evaluative discourse, both moral and aesthetic, by saying that the words used in this type of discourse have emotive meaning. By emotive meaning he means a power or disposition to produce emotional and attitudinal effects on the hearer. Stevenson seems to have been strongly influenced in this direction by his observation that certain words, for example, "nigger", "mongrel", "communist", and "democratic", seem to convey strong emotional attitudes of approval or disapproval.

It seems right to say that evaluative discourse is closely related to attitudes and sentiments in that, in expressing one's judgement of the value of something, one is also expressing an attitude to it, and perhaps also revealing a feeling about it. Furthermore, one makes judgements of value with a view to influencing the behaviour of other people: if they accept one's evaluation of an action or object, they must in consistency act appropriately, seeking it if it is good, avoiding it if it is bad. Stevenson's notion of emotive meaning seems to be capable of explaining both the relationship between value judgements and attitudes and the way value-language is used to influence action, for emotive meaning is the power of words to induce emotional states and attitudes in others, and such states and attitudes naturally affect their actions.

To show that this emotive power of value-words is related to their linguistic function Stevenson has to show that emotive meaning differs in no essential respect from what he calls 'cognitive meaning'. In the causal theory he finds a theory which can easily accommodate his idea of different kinds of meaning by treating such differences as differences in the effects which words have power to produce. Cognitive meaning corresponds with cognitive effects (beliefs and thoughts), emotive meaning with emotive effects (emotions and attitudes).

Associationism. Words produce effects in the mind but of course some words produce more effects than others, and more effect on some people than on others, and these effects may themselves produce effects, and so on. We may introduce the notion of 'associations to a word' to cover all the mental effects a word may produce either directly or indirectly. It now becomes possible to speak of some words, or of words in some contexts, as being particularly rich in meaning, that is, having many associations, and to speak of the metaphorical function of words as depending on the mingling or interaction of associations. It becomes possible to explain differences in the interpretation of, for example, poetry, in terms of differences in personal associations. These are possible ways of talking about meaning if one accepts the causal theory: associations are the effects of words on the mind and according to one version of the causal theory that is what meaning is.

The possibility of elaborating causal theories in these two ways is an attraction. However, in neither case does the elaboration succeed in its object. Evaluative language is not accurately characterised as language whose function is to influence action by causally inducing emotions or attitudes; and neither metaphorical language nor differences in interpretation are to be explained by the notion of associations.

I said earlier in this chapter that an attraction of the causal theory is its apparent ability to answer both what- and how-questions, to say both what meaning is and how words acquire it. It is its pretensions in the latter direction which give it an apparently scientific character. Like another famous philosphical theory, the causal theory of perception, the causal theory of meaning is presented as following naturally from scientific discoveries. In both cases, however, the impression is illusory; in neither case does scientific discovery compel the acceptance of the philosophical theory. It is of course true that words as print, or as sounds, affect our nervous systems and produce effects there. It is also true that the behaviour we call communicating (speaking and understanding) would not occur were these processes not taking place. But it does not follow from this that science can tell us about meaning. Symbols must produce effects in the brain of a mathematician if he is to calculate, but science is not required to give us a theory of mathematics. There are no scientific laws to tell us the meaning of a particular word (this is a conventional matter); though there might well be laws which explained how people came to use a word in a certain way.

The problem with meaning is to discover what we mean by "meaning"; until we have *this* clear we shall not know what scientific investigations will be relevant to the question how words get meanings. The causal theory appears to outline a scientific account of how certain sorts of physical events come to produce certain sorts of mental events. But it could only be a scientific account of the way in which a word acquired a meaning if the meaning of a word were the effects it produces, or the power to produce these effects, and we shall see that it is neither.

Nor can the causal theory be interpreted as a scientific theory of communication. Science investigates empirical relationships; in the case of communication, presumably relationships between the physiological elements of the brain, between these elements and the physical stimuli which affect them, and between physical stimuli and behaviour. But to explain how certain sounds serve as vehicles of communication by saying that they cause or have the power to cause thoughts, beliefs, ideas, etc., would be to say, simply that words affect men's thoughts because they affect or have the power to affect men's thoughts, that they serve to communicate because they serve to communicate. It is a tautology that something which serves to communicate affects or has the power to affect men's thoughts. The causal theory of meaning, then, can no more provide a scientific explanation of communication than the hypothesis that a drug has a dormitive power can explain why it puts us to sleep.

Questions about how we learn to use words and questions about the physical events which occur when we are communicating are proper questions for the scientist, but the questions what it is for a word to have a meaning, and what the meaning of a particular word is, are not.

There is a common feeling that words are poor substitutes for things and that communication would be more accurate and richer if we could in some way use objects (chairs, tables, colours) to communicate instead of words. Communication with words is often regarded as indirect or removed from reality. But the feeling is a mistaken one. If we were to use objects to communicate, they would become like words. They would function like words, and conventions for their use would develop exactly as they have for words (see Chapter 12).

Nevertheless it may be this feeling in part which leads Richards to speak of 'delegated efficacy', to suggest that words are substitutes for things and that our reactions to words are, or should be, like our reaction to the things they are substitutes for. Of course our reactions to words differ enormously from our reactions to the things they are used to refer to; to see this one has only to think of the words "steak" and "woman". It might still be maintained that our reactions on hearing words are *in some respects* like our reactions on seeing things, but in fact no such qualifications will suffice to make this sort of account satisfactory.

The nature of our reactions on hearing a word (to be precise we should speak here of sentences rather than words) depends amongst other things on the grammatical construction we put on it. Words have meanings, but how we take or react to utterances of words depends on whether we regard them as constituting a question, an order, a statement, a request, a piece of advice, or a prediction, and so on. Our reactions to words depend on their grammatical context and even in a single-word language the utterance of any word would have to be taken, or understood, in one or another of these grammatical senses. Speech has a grammar, but objects have not, hence our reactions to objects are not, like our reactions to speech, governed by grammatical conventions. The suggestion that one's reaction on hearing "steak" might resemble one's reaction on perceiving steak looks absurd the moment one realises that the utterance "steak" may be a statement, a question, or a piece of advice, and that the reactions to these will all be different; only grammatical conventions can make it clear which reaction is appropriate.

There is another source of error in the causal theory: this is the idea that understanding a word is reacting in some way to it, so that communication consists in uttering words which cause effects on the thoughts of another person. In the first place, the clearer we are that something is a reaction, the less likely are we to describe it as a case of understanding. We would not describe a reflex knee jerk as an understanding

of the hammer blow. A soldier comes to attention automatically at the command "Attention": his reaction is like a
reflex which he is trained to perform in certain circumstances without thinking, indeed without exercising any
mental faculty.

If all our responses to words were zombie-like or automatic, then we would not speak of understanding utterances:
we do not, after all, speak of a circus horse understanding
the command which produces the conditioned response in
it of tapping so many times with its hoof. Moreover, if the
thoughts in our minds were automatic responses to others'
utterances our thoughts could be controlled by others. On
the one hand, this is not what happens; on the other, if it
were, we would not call it understanding but some sort of
mental reflex.

In the second place, an important distinction has to be
drawn between *causal relations* and *meaning relations*. A
person *A* may utter certain sounds *w* and thereby *cause*
another person *B* to react in a certain way, for example, to
think certain things. Does it follow that *A* *meant* anything
by *w*, or that *w* meant anything or means anything, or that
what it means is to be discovered by observing *B*'s reactions?
None of these things follows. Something can make me
think that something is the case without meaning anything
in the way words mean, and someone can use it to make me
think that something is the case without either its meaning
anything or his meaning anything by it.

Suppose that a man shows me a picture of my wife
embracing another man and as a result I think certain things
about the man and my wife. I may say, "That photograph
means that my wife has been unfaithful". Again, suppose
that a man makes yeti tracks all over my garden and as a

result I think that a yeti has been through the garden. I may say, "These tracks mean that a yeti has passed by". In both cases someone has made use of something, the tracks or the photograph, to make me think something; and in each case I might well have said that the thing (tracks or photograph) *meant* something. Notice, however, that we may say exactly the same thing about clouds and rain, or smoke and fire, that is, that clouds mean rain, and smoke means fire. All that the word "means" means here is that one thing is a a sign of the other in the causal sense: they are causally connected. We would not say that the man who made the tracks, or showed me the photograph, *meant* "a yeti has been here" or "your wife was unfaithful" simply because his action produced this belief; he may have intended nothing of the kind. Nor would we say that the photograph *means* "Xs wife is unfaithful", or that the tracks *mean* "yetis have been here", any more than we would say that clouds mean "it will rain", or smoke "there's a fire". By contrast, if a man says "Jones is ill", I may well think that Jones is ill. In this case I do so not because his saying, "Jones is ill" is causally related to Jones's illness (a sign of it), or because the words "Jones is ill" are causally related to Jones's illness, but because I am familiar with the conventional use of these words; there is a convention which gives these words this sense. We would, accordingly, say in this case both that the speaker meant "Jones is ill" by what he said and that his words mean "Jones is ill".

A thing x may be causally related to a thing y and hence be called a sign of y, i.e. it means, when it occurs, that y is about. Such an x may be used by a person A to make a person B think that y is about. This situation is very different from that in communication in which words convey thoughts not because they are causally related to the things thought about but because they are related by convention to these things. The word "steak" does not mean steak in the way that clouds mean rain; its occurrence is in no way a sign of steak. We might say that clouds are *natural signs* of rain as smoke is of fire, whereas "steak" and "woman" are *conventional signs* for steak and woman.

The causal theory, then, involves a misinterpretation of the concepts of understanding and communicating. The theory, however, is essentially an attempt to define the meaning of a word as its effect in producing, or its power to produce, thoughts or beliefs in the minds of hearers. I want now to show that it cannot be used to define either what it is for a word to have a meaning, or what the particular meaning of a particular word is.

If the theory were correct, then, since many other things besides words produce thoughts and beliefs, many other things besides words could be said to have meaning and to mean things in the way words do, a boot or whip to the kinky, a daffodil to the Wordsworthian, granny's cottage to the child, a worm-eaten carrot to the gardener, and a woman to a man. Although each of these produces, fairly constantly, certain thoughts and feelings, none of them has meaning in the linguistic sense (though all of them may well have meaning in yet another sense to be examined later). Indeed, if the causal accounts were accepted, everything would have meaning, since everything affects someone's thoughts and beliefs in some way. For this reason alone the theory must fail as an attempt to define linguistic meaning. Something which is true of everything is informative about nothing, and cannot be used to define any particular kind of thing such as words.

Moreover, if the causal theory had provided a way of defining linguistic meaning it should also have yielded a technique for deciding how to distinguish the meaning of one word from that of another. If having a meaning is producing thoughts in the mind of a hearer, then the differences in meaning between words ought to correspond to the differences in their effects in the minds of hearers. But here again the causal theory comes to grief. It cannot provide a satisfactory definition of what it is for a particular word to have a particular meaning, for it is impossible to define the meanings of particular words in terms of their effects on hearers.

Words and sentences produce all sorts of effects on thoughts and feelings which have nothing to do with their meaning. The word "athlete" may make us think of a tall man, the word "American" of a rich man, and the word "baby" may make us think of something soft and cuddly. But the thoughts would be irrelevant to the meaning of these words. "American" means "born in, or a naturalised citizen of, the United States of America", "baby" means "very young child", and so on. The difference between "rich" and "born in or naturalised citizen of the United States of America" in relation to "American" comes out in the following way. If I say that Fred is an American though not born in the United States of America, nor a naturalised citizen of that country, I contradict myself, whereas If I say that Fred is rich, and not an American, or American and not rich, I do not. It is a general test of whether a is part of the meaning of b to see whether one can say that x is b but not a without contradicting oneself. If one can, then a is not part of the meaning of b. By this test most of what we think as a result of hearing someone or something described will turn out to form no part of the meaning of the description.

For example, the beliefs we hold about certain things affect what we think when someone talks to us about them. If a novelist writes, "An American walked into the room", we may think—according to our beliefs about Americans, or to our experience of meeting them—of a wealthy, cotton-suited, oil-owning, camera-carrying businessman, or of a sweat-shirted, blue-jeaned hippy. These thoughts could well be called associations to the word "American" or to Americans, but they are not in any sense a part of the meaning of the word "American", nor are they part of what "An American walked into the room" means. If they were, it would be a contradiction in terms to speak of a naked American, or even of an American who wore neither cotton suit nor jeans. If, then someone claims, say in analysing a poem, that in discussing our associations to the words he is discussing the meaning of the poem, he is failing to make this important distinction between meaning and effects. He is failing to distinguish the meaning of words from the various thoughts and beliefs we have about the things the words refer to. I may think about kilts when I hear the word "Scottish", and so may we all, but the word "Scottish" does not include kilts in its meaning.

Assertions about the associations aroused by a particular passage, or line, or word, are empirical hypotheses. They are factual hypotheses about what people associate either with the words or with what the passage, line, or word refers to or is about. Hence it would be necessary to conduct a survey to establish whether people associate wealth with being American, sin with scarlet, innocence with a rose, sorrow with a nightingale, and so on. I do not know to what extent the analysis of poetry ought to be regarded as involving surveys of this kind, (in Chapter 14 there is an example from F. R. Leavis) but if such analyses proceed by hypothesising associations which are not in effect poetic conventions (the associations of innocence and a rose, and sorrow and a nightingale, seem to be cases of special poetic conventions for the use of the words "rose" and "nightingale") they must entail, and wait upon, the result of empirical research.

CONVENTIONS

The meaning of words is governed by convention, not by laws of cause and effect. This is to suggest that there are rules implicit in the use of words, and that it is the use of words according to rules which gives them meaning. That it is not unreasonable to take this view seems clear from the way we criticise language. We speak of the *correct* and *incorrect* use of words and these terms "correct" and "incorrect" normally occur only in relation to rule-governed activities. There may seem a peculiarity here, for clearly the rules according to which we use words cannot be easily formulated in words. But in speaking of rules for using words we imply simply that there are right and wrong ways of using words and that learning the meanings of words is learning to use words in regular and correct ways. The ability to do things in regular or rule-following ways does not entail the ability to say what the rules are, or even the possibility of doing so.

A causal theorist might return to the attack at this point and argue that, of course using a word correctly is using it according to some convention or rule, but the existence of such a convention or rule depends on the word having the power to produce the same effects in different minds on different occasions. The rule merely regularises and codifies this consistency of effect. Such an argument would be completely misplaced. The conventions that govern our use of words are not codifications of cause-and-effect relationships. On the contrary, the way words affect hearers is itself determined by the conventions governing its use. In teaching the meaning of a word we modify people's response to it, we do not change the conventions.

The meaning of a word is entirely a matter of convention and in no way a question of the effects the word may have on a hearer. Consider the case of cricket. When a ball hits the stumps and knocks the bails off, the batsman leaves the field. But what makes him "out" is the existence of a rule or convention of cricket. His leaving the field is only by convention an effect or consequence of the ball hitting his stumps. In general the consequences of events in cricket are determined by the rules of the game, and *these come first*. It would be absurd to suggest that we ought to, or do, wait to see under what circumstances a man is out before we draw up the rules of the game. On the contrary, we draw up the rules and these lay down what effects the events of the game will have. Similarly with words. It would be absurd to suggest that we should wait to see what effects a word produces before deciding the rules for its use. It is the rules which are prior logically. A word's having a meaning can be likened to its having consequences in use which are determined by such rules.

The causal theory of meaning may be looked on as a scientific theory which accounts for that behaviour involving sound and typographic patterns which we call using words with meaning and explains how it is passed on from one person to another. Seen in this light it is plainly too naive to be taken seriously. However, the theory may more reasonably be taken as an attempt to define "meaning" in terms of the effects of words on the minds of hearers, these effects being related to the character of classes of objects. On this interpretation, as we have seen, the theory is radically inadequate.

In view of the criticisms put forward in this chapter one must abandon the causal theory. We may do so, however, and still cling to the view either that the meaning of a word is a mental thing, or that it is a physical thing or set of things. It is these two doctrines which must now be examined.

CHAPTER 11

"FIDO"–FIDO THEORIES
OF MEANING

IT is natural to think of words and meanings as two quite different sorts of things constituting two classes: (1) words, phrases and sentences; (2) meanings, each of the items in the first class being paired off with an item, or perhaps several items, in the second class. To say that this view is natural is not to say that it is on everybody's lips; on the other hand, most people, if asked about meaning, would talk as though they assumed the existence of these two kinds of things and as though they had knowledge of both. More important, they would at the same time assume that the meanings of words are things one can discover or reveal as one can the species to which plants or birds belong. But there are no such things as meanings. There is no class of things corresponding to the second of the categories mentioned above.

It might seem that the existence of dictionaries provides an immediate refutation of this opinion, for surely dictionaries give definitions which constitute the meanings of words. In fact, however, dictionaries are complicated books. They provide a great deal of information about words and a variety of different kinds of information. They tell us the grammatical role of a word, its derivation, the sorts of situations in which it might be used, and perhaps some in which it has been used, and they note other words or phrases which are synonymous with it. Exactly what should be described as 'giving the meaning of a word' will be discussed more fully in Chapter 13. However, it is question-

able whether any of the bits of information provided by dictionaries should be called giving the meaning of a word except in the case where it offers a synonym or synonymous phrase. In such a case a dictionary might state, for example:
– Brother: male child of the same parents, *or*
– Brother: male sibling.
Notice, however, that what is given as the meaning of the word "brother" is simply, in one case, six and, in the other, two, additional words. All we learn from the dictionary is that the word "brother" has the same meaning as "male sibling" or "male child of the same parents". This is one facet of the intuitively obvious fact that one cannot learn a language (as distinct from an abstract calculus) from a dictionary alone. A dictionary just shows us how words are related to one another; it cannot tell us how any given word is related to things in the world unless we already know how certain other words are related to things in the world. A Dutchman, by looking at a dictionary, might gather that "brother" and "male sibling" mean the same, but he might still have no idea what either meant in the sense that he might still have no idea how to use either expression, what things to call brothers, or what things to call male siblings. Dictionaries, then, in so far as they provide meanings for words, provide only more words. Their existence, therefore, gives no support to the view that there is a special class of things called meanings.

There are other things that could be, and have from time to time been, mentioned in reply to the question "What sorts of things are the meanings of words?", or the question "What is the meaning of a word?".

(1) particular objects, events or situations (this chair, this red thing);

(2) classes of objects, events or situations (chairs, red things);

(3) universals, properties or essences (redness, chairness);

(4) mental states, ideas, images or thoughts.

We have strong feelings which incline us to accept one or other of the first three suggestions. On the one hand we feel that our language is related to and reflects actual characteristics in the world, that our words do not have arbitrary meanings but in some sense correspond to the pattern and order which the world displays, so that when, for example, we use the words "red" or "beauty" we are in some way referring to, or drawing the attention of others to, real things such as beauty and redness. On the other hand we feel that when we talk we talk about things, we (as it were) present situations to our hearers, drawing their attention to them by what we say, and that understanding what a person means when he says something is becoming aware of the situation of which he speaks.

Behind the fourth suggestion is the feeling that the meaning of what we say depends on and reflects what we have in mind, and that what we are taken to mean depends on what our hearer has in mind as a result of what we say. One can pursue *this* line of thought even further: what we have in mind and convey in our speech need not, perhaps, correspond to features of the world as it is, only to the world as we see it, so that words reflect not the characteristics of the world but the characteristics of our perception of the world. In this chapter I shall consider the view that the meanings of words are the things we talk about when we use words. In the following two chapters I shall examine the notion of meanings as things in the mind and the notion of meanings as independent and real characteristics of the world. To reject, as I shall, the view that the meanings of words are the things we use words to talk about is not to deny that we use words to talk about things. Nor is it to deny the important role which pointing to objects plays in teaching and learning the meanings of words. Plainly we do use words to talk about the world and we do teach the meanings of many words by pointing out features of the world; indeed the meaning of some words could not be taught in any other way. All this may be conceded and yet the view of meanings as what we use words to talk about dismissed.

THE PICTURE THEORY OF MEANING

One way of looking at language (sometimes called the 'picture theory of meaning') is to regard it as a sort of complex paint-box out of which we make pictures of the world. A sentence pictures a particular situation and the meaning of the sentence is that situation. The meanings of the individual words in the sentence are parts of that situation. Thus, for example:

"The cat is on the mat" means

The relationship between sentence and situation on this theory is quite complex. Some words correspond to *elements* of the situation, typically common nouns, adjectives and verbs, others correspond to the *arrangement* of elements in the situation, for example, "on", "by", "next to" and so on. The arrangement of elements in the situation may be pictured, moreover, not only by particular parts of

the sentence but also by the arrangement of the parts of the
sentence. Thus, for example, "John loves Mary" pictures
one situation and "Mary loves John" a different situation.

Of course the picturing is not to be thought of as natur-
alistic, such as it would be in a photograph or even a painting.
A sentence is not meant to look like the situation which is
its meaning. The representation is intended to be thought
of as conventional, perhaps in the way that a map conventionally represents height by contour lines, towns by
dots, and rivers by blue lines, or a geometric drawing by
similar conventions represents vectors or lines of stress.
Now, it is not to be denied that the sentences we utter have
a relationship to the world. How else would it make sense
to speak of them as informing us or asking us questions
about it? How else would it be possible to speak of pro-
ceeding, by investigation and observation, to decide whether
a given statement is true or false? The question at issue,
however, is, on the one hand, whether the relationship
which certainly exists is to be compared with picturing, and,
on the other, whether what is described as being pictured
by a sentence should be called the meaning of that sentence.

The first and most obvious thing to notice is that sentences
differ enormously from pictures, even conventional pictures
like maps and geometric representations. The latter at least
preserve some of the characteristics of what they represent,
in particular spatial relationships: their mode of representation is not wholly conventional. Language, on the other
hand, is wholly conventional in its relationship to the world,
and it is this which makes the terms "representation" and
"picture" wholly inappropriate in describing the relationship. What possible point could there be in saying, on the
one hand, that "John" represents John and "table" table,

and on the other, that there is absolutely no similarity between "John" and John or "table" and tables, the representation being purely a matter of convention?

The theory may be revised to leave out the notion of picturing or representation, replacing it by the notion of "standing for". In this form we have what Gilbert Ryle has called a "Fido"–Fido theory of meaning: the meaning of a word is what it stands for and the meaning of a sentence the situation it describes. Both the original picture theory and the new "Fido"–Fido theory (so called because it suggests that the meaning of the dog's name "Fido" is the dog Fido) are open to a series of devastating objections. Take, for example, negative sentences. What is the situation which they picture or stand for? Does "The cat is not on the mat" picture, or stand for,

this: or this: or this: ?

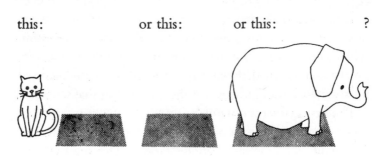

Since, according to the theory, the meaning of the sentence is the situation it stands for, and since the sentence plainly has a meaning, there must be a situation which it stands for. But one can imagine an infinite number of possible situations in which the cat is not on the mat, and it seems absurd to suppose that the meaning of "the cat is not on the mat" is either an infinite disjunction of these (the cat is on the patio, or on the grass, or next door, or running about, etc.) or any *one* of them (it plainly is not, for example, that the cat is in the garden).

Hypothetical sentences present a similar problem. What does "If John is ill, then Mary will be weeping" stand for or picture? One can talk about hypothetical situations but one cannot point to them. A supporter of the picture or "Fido"–Fido theory might say that the hypothetical proposition about John and Mary need not picture or stand for anything since it merely affirms that the two statements, "John is ill" and "Mary will be weeping" are related in a certain way, namely, that if the first is true then the second is also true. This suggestion hardly avoids the difficulty, since a hypothetical proposition may be true and meaningful even when neither of its component clauses reflects any existing situation. Moreover, the suggestion raises a further problem, that of false propositions. It seems that on the picture theory, or the "Fido"–Fido theory, a false proposition should have no meaning, since, being false, it does not represent the facts and there can therefore be no situation of the kind portrayed.

There are then substantial arguments against both the picture and "Fido"–Fido theories of meaning and the arguments seem to indicate clearly that it is a mistake to think of the meanings of words and sentences as the things and situations they are used to talk about. There is, however, a *fundamental* confusion underlying these theories. This is the confusion of *sense* with *reference*.

SENSE AND REFERENCE

Some of the things we say in ordinary conversation suggest that we do think objects in the world to be the meanings of the words we use. Suppose, for example, that I am talking about "the girl at the back of the room".

Someone asks me, "Which girl do you mean?", and I say "That one". It looks as though someone is asking what I mean by "the girl at the back of the room" and that I am replying by pointing to a particular object in the world, i.e. a girl. Indeed we say such things as "I meant that one when I said 'the girl, etc.'" It seems reasonable, then, to say that the phrase "the girl at the back of the room" meant or means *that* object, and that the object was or is its meaning. Many other examples of this kind could be constructed. They all depend, however, on an ambiguity in the word "means". One ambiguity in this word has already been pointed out. We use it in connection sometimes with natural signs, sometimes with conventional signs:
– Clouds mean rain, *or*
– "Brother" means "male sibling".
We are now faced with another ambiguity in "means": we use the word sometimes in talking about the *sense* of an expression and sometimes in talking about the *reference* of an expression. Questions of the form: Did you mean that animal or person, etc?, Which animal or person did you mean?, Which thing did you mean by the words ...?, are all questions about the reference of an expression. They are not questions about its meaning or sense.

For example, suppose that I say in the course of conversation, "His brother is a cad". I may be asked two kinds of question:

(1) "What does that mean?"; to which a possible answer would be "His male sibling is a cad", or "His brother is a rotter, a poor type, an uncivilised and immoral bounder, etc., etc." The questioner asks the question because he fails

to understand the meaning of one or other of the words I have used, in the sense that these are bits of the English language which he has failed to master. He displays a lack of linguistic skill and in my reply I repair the gap by teaching him the meaning or sense of one or other of the expressions I have used.

(2) "Who (which one) do you mean?"; to which a possible answer would be "His *younger* brother" or "*That* fellow over there". In this case the questioner knows the language; he is not ignorant of bits of English and does not need to be taught the meanings of words. His problem is that I have not made quite clear to him which person I am talking about, and I answer his question by replacing one way of referring to a man ("*his* brother") by another which is perhaps more specific, or more direct.

This example should make it quite clear that questions about meaning (sense) are quite different from questions about who, or which thing, is meant (reference). It is to be noticed that questions about meaning (sense) are questions about the use of a word in general, whereas questions about reference are questions about the intention of a particular speaker in making a particular utterance. Moreover, questions about reference will normally arise only in the case of expressions the sense of which is already known.

One may say "He is a delightful chap", and the man one means (is referring to) may be the Duke of Edinburgh. But "he" does not mean the same as "the Duke of Edinburgh". If one is inclined to suggest that in this sentence at least "he" means the same as "the Duke of Edinburgh", then one is either committed to the view that "he" has an infinite number of meanings, a different one each time it is used to refer to a different person, which is absurd, or one is simply saying that "he" in *this* sentence *refers* to the Duke of Edinburgh. It is a standard characteristic of speech that a word having a constant meaning may be used to refer to many different particular things. Phrases like "the cow" have a different reference almost every time they are used, but their meaning remains the same. Indeed one can see that this must be so, for, if it were not, the phrase "the cow" would have to function like a proper name: one could not tell what it meant on any occasion unless one had first been introduced. Clearly this is not the case. Even though one can be unclear exactly which cow is being referred to on odd occasions, one always knows what *kind* of animal is in question. One can also find phrases and words with different meanings and the same reference. The expressions "that man", "he", "the gamekeeper", and "Lady Chatterley's lover" might all have the same reference although they plainly do not all have the same meaning.

The temptation to think of the meanings of words as objects arises, it seems, from a desire to understand how words connect with things in the world. This temptation is enormously increased by the fact that we use the word "means" to ask questions not only about meaning but also about reference. The whole matter is further confused by the fact that, although the meaning of a word in a particular utterance is not a particular object in the world, when it comes to defining *identity* of meaning one possible suggestion is that two words have the same meaning if, and only if, all the objects which may be properly referred to by them are the same. I shall leave the problem of identity at this stage, remarking only that, while the problem of what it is for two words to mean the same is intimately connected with the problem of what it is for a word to have a meaning, it is not connected with the spurious question, "what are meanings?" One may accept that words have meanings and deny that there are such things as meanings.

The arguments against the two other suggestions mentioned earlier in the chapter, that the meaning of a word may be a *class* of objects, or else an abstract idea are interesting and complex, but I shall note only one or two of them briefly. The suggestion that the meaning of the word "cat" is cats clearly has some of the weaknesses of the "Fido"–Fido theory. It cannot be correct since it implies that the proposition "There are no cats" is, if true, meaningless. It is difficult to see how a proposition can be meaningful when false and meaningless when true. Moreover how could one tell that a proposition was true if it were meaningless? The only possible way out of this weird dilemma would be to maintain that "Cats exist" is a necessary truth and that therefore "There are no cats" is a contradiction. But this is clearly absurd.

Further if the meaning of "cat" were an object or class of objects (e.g. a cat or the class of cats), it would make sense to attribute properties applicable to such objects to the meaning of "cat" and vice versa. But this is not in general the case. We speak of cats dying and of the species becoming extinct, but we do not speak of the meaning of "cat" dying or becoming extinct. Similarly a cat, but not the meaning of "cat" may have fur, be affectionate, or love Kit-e-Kat. And the meaning of "cat" but not a cat, may be stated or mis-stated by Fred, defined by William or learned by Mary.

Lastly, the meaning of the word "cat" cannot be an abstract cat or the abstract idea of a cat. Bishop Berkeley, long ago, in attacking the abstractionism of Locke, pointed out that it is impossible to conceive of an abstract triangle, a figure which is three-sided but not isosceles, or scalene, or equilateral, or right-angled. Similarly a cat which is not ginger, or black, or white, or marmalade, not Persian or Siamese or Manx, neither longhaired nor shorthaired, neither tailless nor tailed, and so on, is equally impossible. The notion of an abstract cat is absurd, and hence the suggestion that the meaning of "cat" is an abstract cat, or an abstract idea of cat, is absurd.

CHAPTER 12

UNDERSTANDING AND KNOWING
THE MEANING OF WORDS

W E are inclined to think that understanding the meaning of
a word or sentence is simply experiencing a mental state or
event (thought, idea or image) which occurs when we hear
the word or sentence. It follows, we may also think, that
knowing the meaning of a word is being acquainted with
these mental states or events. Locke thought of communication in this light. One person uses words to stand for the
ideas in *his* mind which, on being heard by another, give
rise to ideas in *his* mind. The second person understands the
first if his ideas on hearing the words correspond with those
the speaker had in mind on uttering them.

It is certainly true that, instead of speaking of one person
understanding what another says, one commonly speaks of
someone grasping, or getting, the idea another has in mind
and one speaks also of someone conveying the idea he has in
mind. Moreover one speaks of 'flashes' of comprehension
and of '*seeing*' what is meant, again as though understanding
the meaning of something were possessing or experiencing
some mental object or event. One can, however, be misled
by these ways of speaking. Ideas and thoughts, in the sense
in which we speak of them being conveyed or grasped, are
not in fact mental events at all. To say that a book is full of
good ideas is not to say that it is full of mental things, rather
that it contains statements and suggestions which are
interesting. Ideas in this sense of "idea" may be possessed by
several people. "There are human beings on other planets"

is an idea and if two people both think it, then they think of the same idea. But ideas in the sense of mental events cannot be shared. Smith cannot convey to Jones the events in his own mind.

Again, when we speak of seeing in a flash what someone means we do not necessarily imply that we have had a visual experience. It may just be that we feel sure at the time that we can explain, or express what he meant. Having such thoughts is like seeing, for when we see something, a view from a window, or along a street, we feel, and we often are suddenly in a position to say a great many things about what we see. So, too, when we think we understand something we feel suddenly in a position to say and express a great deal concerning what we believe we understand. This sudden feeling of an accession of power to talk about something is common to seeing and to many instances of understanding, and it explains the analogical use of the word "see" in speaking about understanding. But the differences are great, and we should not be misled into thinking, because we speak of seeing what is meant, that meaning is something we experience, or are aware of in our minds, that it is something there in the mind to be perceived if we attend closely.

There is a further reason why we may be inclined to think of understanding the meaning of something as a mental event. Words after all are just noises, or groups of marks on paper. Yet understanding them is thinking about objects such as trees, people and colours. How are we to comprehend a person reacting in this way to noises and marks if we do not think of him as having mental images or ideas which, it seems, are much more closely related to the objects he thinks about? Must not understanding a word be a matter of transforming it, or of translating it, into some intuitively comprehensible thing like an image? Must not the meaning of the word, therefore, be some such image in the mind?

Suppose that I say to Mirabelle "Bring me a red apple", and she goes and gets one. Unable to explain to myself how these sounds I uttered could have had this consequence, I may ask, "How did you know that this apple was the sort I meant by 'red'? How did you know which action to perform when I said 'bring'? How did you know which apple to pick?" Mirabelle might reply as follows: "It's quite simple. I heard the word 'red' and I have learnt to associate 'red' with a red image. I heard the word 'apple' and I have learnt to associate this word with an image of an apple, etc. So when I heard 'red apple' I called up in my mind the image of a red apple and then I picked out an object resembling this image."

If the view of meaning as a mental event and of understanding as experiencing such a mental event were correct, this sort of reply would be satisfactory. But it is not satisfactory, and this can be demonstrated quite simply. We have merely to ask how Mirabelle knew that the image she called up was an image of a red apple; how she knew, in other words, that her image was the correct or appropriate image. Did she need another image to compare it with, and, if she did not, then why should she need an image at all? If she can tell without the aid of further images that a given image is an image of a red apple, why should she need an image in the first place to decide whether a given *object* is a red apple? Mirabelle's explanation gives rise to a dilemma for the proponents of the theory we are considering. Either she needs an image to enable her to recognise a red apple, in which case she must need a further image to help her recognise the image of a red apple, and a still further image to recognise that image, and so on ad infinitum; or she needs no image at all.

Should Mirabelle explain how she understands my request not in terms of images but in terms of thoughts or beliefs, a similar argument applies. For suppose that when I make my request she thinks to herself the words, "I am to bring a red apple"; the same problem arises again. Does Mirabelle need another thought to understand this thought (this sentence), and, if so, yet another to understand that one? If she does not, then she does not need the first thought in order to understand my request to her. If she can understand the sentence *she says to herself* mentally without further mental sentences, then she can understand the sentence *I say to her* without any mental sentences at all.

An objection might be raised here. Mirabelle has no need to recognise that her image is an image of a red apple; the question whether the image she has is of the right sort is not one that she needs to ask. The image can be supposed to occur automatically and her action to follow automatically. But, if she can be supposed to act automatically in response to an image, she can also be supposed to act automatically in response to words spoken to her. There is no need, then, to introduce images or thoughts in order to explain how she knows what to do when asked for a red apple.

But of course images are introduced into the account of what it is to understand the meanings of words largely because our actions in response to words are not automatic. We hear a request, understand it, and then decide whether to act on it or not. We have considered the problem of how, in terms of this theory, a person tells whether or not his image is the right sort of image (whether or not, for example, it is an image of a red apple.) Now we must turn to a second major problem, that of the interpretation of images or other mental states.

The inclination to describe understanding in terms of mental events arises from a feeling that some things, such as words, need interpretation if we are to act on them, whereas others, such as images and thoughts, do not: they are intrinsically comprehensible. Thus understanding the meaning of words is presented as a process of translating what is not intrinsically (but only conventionally) comprehensible into something mental which *is* intrinsically comprehensible. The error in this line of thought lies in supposing that anything is intrinsically comprehensible, that there are things which are incapable of being misunderstood, or misinterpreted. Suppose that when I said "Bring me a red apple" Mirabelle had one of the following complex images:

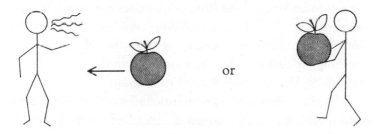

or

Each of these complex images is itself capable of being interpreted in numerous ways. Does

mean: protect me from, protect someone else from, bring here, carry away, carry forward, carry backward, or pray for? Does the sign

mean: bring, take, look at, is coming, or is going?

No set of symbols is incapable of misinterpretation. Hence it is impossible to maintain that a person understands one set of symbols by converting them into another set of symbols, unless we add that he understands the second set without translating it. But in that case there is no reason why he should not have understood the first set without translating it. Either one needs a further set of symbols to understand a given set, in which case one needs an infinite number of sets to understand the first; or one does not need any such further set. But if understanding symbols involved an infinite number of translations we should understand nothing. It follows then, since we do understand what is said to us, that we do not need to translate it.

The plausibility of the mentalistic theory of understanding and meaning is not improved if instead of symbolic images one hypothesises a life-like or cinema-like sequence of pictures. Suppose that when I say "Bring me a red apple", Mirabelle has a cinema-like experience of herself bringing me a red apple. Can she misinterpret this? Of course she can. For why should she take her imaginings for an indication that she is to *do* something rather than as information about the past, or as a prediction about the future or simply as a set of pictures. Could she not, on the other hand, if she does take what I say as a request, take it as a request not for a red apple but for any apple whatever, or simply for a piece of fruit? Consider what the difference in the pictures would have to be to convey a request for fruit rather than for a specific fruit of a specific colour. The pictures could, in fact, not show a piece of fruit without showing a specific kind of fruit. In other words, the distinction between the specific and the general cannot be made in pictures. No picture, no matter how detailed, could free Mirabelle from this kind of uncertainty in interpreting it. These considerations show how unsatisfactory it is to suppose that some mental translations of sentences carry, as it were, their meaning on their face. They also demonstrate the inadequacy of pictures compared with language. There is much that can be said in words which cannot be represented in pictures.

However speculation about imagery or other mental events is really irrelevant to the question whether or not someone understands or knows the meaning of something. Consider the case of a man who agrees absolutely with us that this and that and that are chairs and that this and that and the other are tables, and so on. He never disagrees with us, and we are never surprised to find him calling a chair a table, or a desk a chair. Along comes a second man who says "I know he always uses the word 'table' in the same way and of the same things as we do, and I am sure he always will. Nevertheless, he still does not know the meaning of the word, and does not mean the same by it as we do, for he has quite the wrong image when he uses it". This objection is absurd. We do not decide whether or not a man uses a word correctly—or discover what he means by it—by investigating his imagery. We observe whether he uses it in the same way as we do, whether he calls the same things as we do tables, chairs, desks and so on.

The theory that the meanings of words are images and

that understanding is a mental process involving images implies that we can not ever tell whether a person uses a word correctly, or understands its meaning, unless we know what images occur to him when he utters or hears it. We cannot of course observe his imagery directly so that we can only learn about it from his description of it. However, if the theory is correct, since we cannot know what his description means until we know what images he has when he speaks, his descriptions must always be meaningless. We need to know what images he has in order to know what he means when he describes his images to us. But we cannot know what images he has except from his description. Plainly the situation is irresolvable. The final consequence of the theory must be that we can never know whether other people mean the same as we do, by the words they use and that consequently we can never tell whether they use words correctly or not. This is a logical consequence of the theory, and it is plainly false. It follows that the theory itself is false.

The theory of meaning as images or other mental states originates in part from a mistaken view of understanding and knowing the meaning of a word as certain sorts of mental experience. One is tempted to think in this way, for we speak of a person understanding immediately, and knowing what someone meant immediately, as though the knowing and the understanding were mental events which occurred at a certain time in response to what was said. But knowing and understanding are not events. If they were then the question whether a person understood or knew the meaning of a word on a particular occasion could be settled by examining that occasion alone, and this is not the case. Suppose a man is playing tennis and returns the first service low across the net to the far corner of the service court; can one decide from this that he knows how to play tennis? If all his subsequent shots are feeble and erratic, we must reassess his first forehand return as a lucky shot rather than as the exercise of a skill. Similarly, a man might, when I say "*Fermez la porte*", shut the door. Shall I conclude from this that he understands French; or is there anything else I could know about his behaviour at the time from this would follow? The answer is that I may think at the time that he understands, but, if on later occasions he completely fails to act appropriately and uses French in an erratic manner, I must reassess his initial performance as coincidental or lucky rather than as the exercise of linguistic skill.

Understanding and knowing the meaning of words is using them correctly and responding appropriately when others use them. The concepts of understanding and knowing the meaning of a word refer to patterns of behaviour, in particular, skills exhibited over fairly long periods. We may well say that someone understands the meaning of a word on a particular occasion, but in doing so we are hypothesising that his behaviour on that occasion is an exercise of a skill. If his later behaviour shows that he does not possess this skill, if he fails to respond to the word correctly and is unable to use it discriminatingly, our original judgement must be revised. In teaching a child to talk, one is often persuaded that he knows the meaning of a word, say "Daddy", because he calls his father Daddy, only to discover that this judgement was incorrect because he also calls other males, and the odd female too, Daddy.

One can draw distinctions between three kinds of knowledge, knowing that something is the case, being able to do something (knowing how to do it) and knowing some person, place or thing. The first of these forms of knowledge is knowledge of propositions or truths, and the last is acquaintance with something (having met or seen it). Understanding and knowing the meaning of words is being able to use them and respond to them; it is neither knowledge of truths nor acquaintance with things, mental or otherwise. The correct answer to the question how we understand words and their use is that we learn these skills from those who teach us to speak. How this process occurs is a complex problem for psychologists. It is not to be solved by postulating acquaintance with 'mental meanings'.

The account of understanding and knowing the meanings of words as skills or the exercise of skills seems to me to be substantially correct. However, it does raise problems and difficulties. In particular it poses the question how long a person must go on using a word correctly before we can say he understands its meaning. There are really two problems here:

(1) If a man uses a word correctly once, and thereafter incorrectly, one says that the first occasion was a case of luck. If he uses it correctly for years and then starts using it incorrectly one says that he did originally know the meaning, but has forgotten it. Where should one draw the line between these cases? At what point in time can one say that, if from then on a man consistently uses a word incorrectly it will be an indication not that he has never known how to use it, but that he did once and has now forgotten? There is, I think, no abstract, or *a priori* answer to this question. One must decide on a rough and ready estimate of the probability of using words correctly by chance, and on one's general experience of the phenomena of forgetting.

(2) A man may use a word as we do for a time and then suddenly use it incorrectly, not because he was just guessing

and his luck turned, nor because he has forgotten, but because all along he meant something different by the word. (He was really using it differently from us all the time.) One knows of men who use colour words and appear to use them correctly, but who in certain circumstances make mistakes. It turns out that they are colour-blind and are using the words in response to the luminosity of objects rather than to differences in colour. How long must someone go on using a word as we do before we can decide that he is really not using it differently? The answer here is that he may always be using it differently, while appearing to use it as we do (and will show this if subjected to appropriate tests). But unless one can think of a specific hypothesis about what the difference is, for example, that he uses colour words in response to luminosity differences, the hypothesis that there is a difference in use is vacuous. When teaching a child it makes sense to wonder, even though he calls cars cars, whether he may be using "car" as we use "vehicle", that is, to cover lorries and buses. One can then test this. But to wonder in general whether someone might really be using a word in a different way from oneself without some specific hypothesis in mind, is like wondering how many things there are in a room without specifying what kind of thing. It is vacuous wondering.

In this chapter and the last it has been argued that meanings are not a sort of thing, that there are no such things as meanings either mental or physical. It is useful to think of the meaning of a word as its use, the way people use it, and of differences in meaning as differences in these uses. Correspondingly one can think of understanding or knowing the meaning of a word as knowing how to use it and understanding how others use it. Crudely, one can think of a word as a tool with a certain use, and of knowing its meaning as having the appropriate skill in using it. However, as we shall see in Chapter 15, it is almost as difficult to define what it is for a word to have a use as it is to define what it is for a word to have a meaning.

CHAPTER 13

MEANING AND DEFINITION

I T seems reasonable to ask why we use the words we do and why we use them as we do, for it seems reasonable to suppose that such questions might be answered, and answered in interesting ways. After all our language is not arbitrary; it obviously functions well; one is even tempted to say that it fits the world rather closely. It ought to be possible to say why we have it or use it. But questions about why we use particular words, when we should use a particular word, and what we use particular words for, are not as straight-forward as they appear to be, or as would be the equivalent questions about, for example augers, or motor cars. Questions of the latter sort may yield informative answers but the former appear always to yield trivial answers. Take the question "When should one use the word 'dog' "? Assuming that the standard we are employing is not one of etiquette but of correct linguistic behaviour, it seems that the answer must be "To talk about dogs", and cannot be "To talk about cats" or any such alternative. Again, in reply to the question "What do we use the word 'dog' for?" we must give an answer such as "To talk about dogs", and rule out any such answer as "To talk about cats". In each case one answer seems to be correct, but trivial and uninformative and all other answers seem to be wrong. The statement, " 'Dog' (if it is used to talk about anything) is used to talk about dogs", made by one who both mentioned and used the word "dog", would be trivially true, its denial self-defeating. It might be objected that, " 'Dog' is used to talk about dogs", could not be a trivial truth, since "Les Anglais emploient le mot 'dog' pour parler des chiens", is clearly not. But one must be careful of translations which ignore unstated implications. The statement, "The French use 'dog' and only 'dog' to talk about dogs" is false, but its translation "Les Français emploient seulement le mot 'dog' pour parler des chiens", is absurd. Anyone who understood this statement and knew it to be in French would know it to be false. Similarly anyone who understood English and knew that " 'Dog' is used to talk about dogs" was in English would know it to be true.

Finally, to the question "Why does one use the word 'dog'?" one might answer "Because there are dogs", and at first sight this looks more interesting. It seems to find a justification for, or explanation of, the existence of the word "dog" in the existence of a category of things, namely dogs. But if the species 'dog' became extinct we would still talk about dogs as we do about dodos. Even if dogs had never existed we could still talk about them as we do about unicorns. Of course, if the question why we use the word "dog" is a scientific one then the answer must be long and complicated. If, however, it requires us to justify the existence of the word "dog", then the answer cannot be that dogs exist, for we might well talk about dogs even if there were none. The only possible justification seems to be that people find a use for the word, presumably to talk about dogs (whether existing or non-existing). So we arrive again at the answer we examined above: the word "dog" is used to talk about dogs.

It is a mistake to think that we can in general use a description of the way things are in the world to explain or justify our having and using the words we do have and use. Such a description will employ the very words we are trying to justify and explain, so that it will be trivially true that the things we describe tally with the language we use to describe them. Nevertheless we are still inclined to feel that more than mere trivialities can be gained from questions about why we use the words we do use. I turn now to two ways in which this feeling can lead us into trouble.

ESSENCES

We all know how to use words. We do not get confused about what to call a cow and what a dog, when to call a person happy and when sad. We have, moreover, the feeling that our discriminating use of words corresponds to real divisions between kinds of things in the world, and that we ought to be able to point out a pattern in the world as an explanation of and justification for using words as we do. It seems to us that because we know how to use words we must know something about the things in the world which correspond to them; that because we can use words discriminatingly, this word for this sort of thing, that for that, we must be aware in our discriminations of essential differences between different sorts of things. If we did not know such distinguishing characteristics of things how would we know which words to apply to which things? It is almost as though we thought of things in the world as having their names written on them—not in letters, of course, but, say, in properties or characteristics.

Sometimes we actually ask ourselves questions apparently about this underlying pattern in the world:

- I call things dogs, horses, and cows, but what are the essential differences between these things?
- What is the essential difference between a vegetable and a fruit?

– Is a person really just two things, a body and a mind?
– What makes a cow a cow?
– What exactly is happiness, or democracy?
– What is the essence of love, life, tragedy or humour?
– Is tragedy really different from comedy; are living things
  really different from machines?

We feel that we ought, by answering these questions, to be able to show whether or not the different uses of two words can be justified by real differences in things, and whether or not a single word ought to be replaced by two because it covers two sorts of things. Such answers ought, we feel, to reveal the essential differences between things which our ability to use words seems to imply we know about and can recognise.

Let us take as an example the question whether machines can think or feel. This problem has arisen because many psychologists and philosophers are disposed to think of people as complex machines while others reject this view on the ground that machines cannot think or feel. We tend to approach the problem as though we knew the essential characteristics of thinking and feeling without being able quite to express them clearly. We feel that if we *could* define them, then we would be able to say straight off either that machines can think or feel, or that they can't. Our apparent ability to be certain in many cases which kinds of things think and which do not (for example, people think; rocks and trees do not) suggests to us that we know of a general or essential difference between thinking and non-thinking things, and that we can therefore apply this knowledge to the case of complex machines.

This attitude to the problem embodies a mistake. Knowing the meanings of words is not in general knowing the essences of things. For what would it be to know the essence of something? Presumably it would be to know, in the case of thinking, that thinking essentially involves the occurrence of x, y and z, or, in the case of feeling, that it essentially involves the occurrence of w, t and v, or, less abstractly, that a fruit is something with properties a, b and c, a vegetable something with d, e and f. However, to say that anything with a, b and c is a fruit, and anything lacking one or more of these properties is not a fruit, is to say that a, b and c are necessary and sufficient conditions of a thing being a fruit, and this in turn is to say that a, b and c make up the definition of the word "fruit". In short, to know about essences would in effect be to know the definitions of words.

It turns out then that, if we suppose that knowing the meanings of words involves knowing the essences of things, we are supposing no more than that knowing the meaning of words is knowing definitions. However, as will be argued throughout this chapter, it is a mistake to think of knowing the meaning of a word 'x' as knowing necessary and sufficient conditions of a thing being x, in other words knowing the definition of 'x'. Knowing how to use a word is not having this sort of knowledge, and in general it could not be. We use words correctly of certain things and not others, but in general we are, and must be, unable to *say* in virtue of what properties of these things our usage is correct or incorrect. To know what properties a thing has is to know what words may be correctly applied to it, and it would be absurd to suggest that in general we can only know that a word applies to a thing if we have already decided what other words apply to it. This would make the use of any word impossible.

Our problem in deciding whether machines can think, or whether a tomato is a fruit or a vegetable, is not to discern an exact and precise recipe for allocating these terms in order to apply them appropriately, for there are in general no such exact recipes. It is to make a decision about a borderline case. Some people will feel the differences (between tomatoes and peaches or between the activities of computers and people) greater than the similarities, others the reverse. Who is correct is not to be decided by thought or investigation; the issue is not a theoretical one but a matter of waiting to see how the language develops. If people eventually *do* call a tomato a fruit, or say that machines think, then that will be correct. Problems arise in deciding when a word is being applied in the same sense to a new class of objects and when it has acquired a new sense. But they are too complex to be dealt with here.

JUSTIFYING THE USE OF WORDS

One has the feeling that knowing the meaning of a word involves knowing why one uses it on particular occasions and hence knowing how to justify one's use of it on these occasions. If one knows the meaning of the word "fruit" and someone asks why one calls some particular object a fruit, one feels one should be able to answer. Moreover, there is an abstract argument which seems to imply that the feeling is correct. Language is transmitted by teaching; indeed language would not exist were this not possible. Now surely if a man A teaches a man B to use a word 'x', A must be able to tell when B uses 'x' correctly, and this appears to imply that he must be able to observe what B uses 'x' of or applies 'x' to. Moreover, it seems there must be certain characteristics of the objects to which B applies 'x' which A can pick out and in virtue of which he will accept or reject B's uses of 'x'. Reference to such characteristics should, therefore, enable one to justify the use of 'x' on a particular occasion.

There are two assumptions in this argument. One is that a word can be meaningful only if we are able to explain its meaning by teaching someone else to use it. The other is that for it to be teachable there must be certain observable characteristics of the things to which a word is applied, in virtue of which it is correctly applied in these cases. The first assumption is correct; it is the second which leads us into difficulties.

Suppose that a person A teaches a person B to use the word "pain", and suppose also that the second assumption is correct. Plainly A cannot observe B's feeling of pain. The most that he can observe is B's circumstances and his behaviour in these circumstances. It follows that he can only justify his using the word "pain" of B by reference to B's behaviour and circumstances. Further, since this is all that A can observe by way of characteristics of B, he must in effect teach B to use the word "pain" of himself when he is in these particular circumstances and behaving in this particular way. Thus, for all A knows, B will learn to use "pain" to refer to his behaviour and circumstances rather than to his pain feelings; indeed he may not have any pain feelings. The argument leads us to conclude that no one can possibly learn to use the word "pain", or any other word or expression for pain feelings, or refer to pain feelings, even when speaking about himself. But this conclusion must be false, for, if this were not possible then we could not state the conclusion itself. Included in it, after all, is an expression which must be understood as referring to pain feelings if the sentence is to make sense, namely the expression "pain feelings".

Where the conclusion of an argument is false, one of the premises must be false. In this case it is the assumption that one must be able to say why one uses a word, to justify its use by indicating *something else* in virtue of which that use is appropriate or correct. If this assumption were right one would have to be able to state necessary and sufficient conditions for the use of all words, and this would imply being able to define all words. In fact, generally speaking, we can do neither.

LEARNING THE MEANING OF A WORD

There are basically two ways in which we can teach a person the meaning of a word: by giving a definition (this is always verbal tuition) and by showing him things (this may be done by pointing, or it may be done verbally).

Demonstrative Teaching. The most common way of teaching someone the use or meaning of a word consists in pointing and saying the word while he observes and listens. We all learn the common nouns and adjectives, "table", "horse", "house", "man", "red", etc. in this way. This is not to be thought of as a kind of definition by pointing, for each case of pointing and saying a word can be misinterpreted or misunderstood. For example, a teacher may point at a red pencil and say the word "red", but the pupil may take him to be indicating not the colour but the shape or the function of the pencil. Over a number of occasions such interpretations will reveal themselves in utterances of the word "red" which the teacher indicates to be incorrect and as a result they will tend to be eliminated. As his pupil acquires a larger vocabulary the teacher may use *words* to point, saying, for example, that yellow is *the colour of primroses*, or lugubrious *the expression on Bill's face*. But there is nothing in the procedure which suggests that he should be able to explain verbally how or when to use the word he is teaching.

Teaching by Definition. To give a definition is to give a word or phrase which is synonymous with the word being defined. For example, "brother" is definable as male sibling, "champagne" as a sparkling white wine from the Champagne area. Such a definition can only be used to teach someone the meaning of a word if he already knows the meaning of the synonym, for the definition supplies a meaning for the word only in the sense that it gives another word or phrase having the same meaning. To be told that two things x and y are the same in respect of some property, for example height or colour, is to be told nothing about the height or colour of either x or y unless the height or colour of one is already known. Similarly one cannot learn the meaning of one word by means of a definition unless one already knows the meaning of at least *some* other word or phrase. It follows that definition-giving cannot be the main way of teaching or learning the meaning of words.

The only sense in which we can *say* what the meaning of a word is, that is *state* the meaning, is by giving a definition. And the only way in which we can produce something which can properly be called the meaning of a word is by saying what the meaning is. But in giving a definition, we supply the meaning of a word 'x' only in the sense that we offer a word 'y' which has the same meaning. One then has two words with the same meaning, but if anyone asks what the meaning they both have is, there is no answer. Moreover, most words do not have exact definitions. This must be obvious when we think that only a language with an enormous redundancy of vocabulary could contain synonyms or synonymous phrases for more than a few words.

It seems then, on the one hand, that stating the meaning of a word, saying what it is, is something which we can only do rather rarely, that is, when there exist synonyms or synonymous phrases; on the other, that even producing a synonymous word or expression is not in a sense revealing the meaning of the word, but merely indicating its identity with the meanings of other words.

It might seem that we do not need to give a definition in order to explain verbally how a word is used, or what its meaning is. We will always find, however, either that such explanations tell us the meaning, in which case they also give us definitions, or that they do not give us definitions, in which case they do not tell us the meaning. I may say, for example, that we use "champagne" of wines which are white and sparkling and come from the Champagne district of France, or that we use "triangle" of plain figures with three straight sides. In each case I am apparently describing the sort of situation in which these words would be used correctly, but in each case my description could be re-phrased as a definition:

- Triangle: a plain figure having three straight sides.
- Champagne: a sparkling white wine from the Champagne district of France.

Compare the case in which I say that we use the word "table" of a piece of furniture for eating off or writing on. Plainly this does not correspond to a definition. Many things which we eat off and write on are not tables. But neither is it an adequate explanation of the meaning of the word "table". In some ways it is too broad and in others too narrow: on the one hand desks are not tables and on the other coffee-tables are.

It was said earlier that most words do not have exact definitions, and this raises the general question how one can tell whether or not a word has a definition. The answer seems to be that one can only tell by investigation, by searching for a definition, and either succeeding or failing. There is, however, a test of success. If a is definable as b then it is impossible for any particular thing x to be a and not b, or b and not a. The suggested definition "Table; a surface supported by legs holding food during meals" fails by this test, for many things are tables of which the suggested definition is not true, and vice versa. The reader may discover by experiment that few words have definitions. He should try, for example, to define the words "aeroplane", "chair", "house", and "red".

Many words can, however, be given *partial* definitions:
- Red: a colour of type x.
- Table: furniture of type y.
- Car: a vehicle of type z.
- Dog: an animal of type w.

Here we have instances of words the meaning of which we can begin to explain in other words. But we cannot complete the task, for we have nothing to put in place of the letters x, y, z and w.

The fact that most words in ordinary language cannot be defined is sometimes taken to imply imprecision in ordinary language. This too is a mistake, for the existence or non-existence of definitions has nothing to do with the precision or vagueness of language. This must be so since a definition simply gives us another word or phrase having the same meaning as the first. It provides us with two words or two phrases instead of one, both having the same meaning. But how could this show that one has, or both have, a *precise* meaning? Perhaps they both have the same vague meaning. The association between precision and definition comes about because it is an advantage for disputants in argument to make sure that they are using words in the same way; attempts at definition may make it clear whether or not this is so. But the question whether or not the word "table" is definable is not related to the question whether or not it is a precise term.

DEFINITION AND ESSENCE

The notions of definition and essence go together. The essence of something is that which makes it what it is, and wherever we can say what makes something what it is we shall be able to give a definition. For example, if we ask what makes a triangle what it is, the answer is being a three-sided plain figure. The fact that most words do not have definitions, then, implies that most things do not have essences. Although one may feel strongly that there is an essential difference between chairs and tables, or between people and machines, the only essential difference, if there is one, is that chairs are chairs and tables tables; people are people and machines machines. If one looks for a set of properties of chairs which are essential to chairs and to chairs alone, and a corresponding set for tables, one will not find them. This is only to be expected, for the objects we use words to talk about are constantly changing (think of the changes in the style of furniture), and our interests change also (what we once regarded as similar we may now want to regard as heterogeneous, for example, bacteria and viruses). For these reasons there are bound to be considerable variations in the properties of objects called by one name at different times. Moreover, at any given time we shall find things called by one name (for example games) which have no common properties (properties possessed by all games). Although each game is similar to *some* other game in *some* respect, the respects in which two games are similar will vary from one pair of games to another.

Part of the reason why we expect to find definitions and essences is that we regard knowing the meaning of a word as knowing about something, or being acquainted with something, which will guide us in our use of the word. We have seen how this view is mistaken when the guide is thought of as an image. It is equally mistaken when the guide is thought of as a definition. This is not just because most words do not have exact definitions, but because *all* our word-using *could* not be guided by other word-using. It cannot be necessary to knowing the meaning of a word that one knows a definition which guides one's use, for being guided by a definition itself involves knowing the meaning of some words. It must be possible to know the meanings of *some* words without ever knowing definitions of them.

Knowing the meaning of a word is not knowing about something which could be presented or described verbally, a definition or an essence; it is not knowing about a thing of any kind. Knowing how to use a word, like knowing how to cast a fly, is not knowing about some special kind of object. Like knowing how to play tennis or swim, it is a skill.

METAPHOR

The arguments presented above have consequences for the notion of metaphor. A metaphor is held to be an *extended* use of a word. Now, to speak of the extended use of a word implies that we are able to speak of a *non-extended* or *central* use. The difference between them could perhaps be explained as follows. The central use conforms to some definition, or to some notion of what is essential to a thing described by the word. The extended use occurs when some of the essential properties are lacking, or when certain conflicting properties are present. But it has been argued that we cannot say, for most words, what are the essential characteristics of things to which they apply, for there are none. But if we cannot, for most words, characterise an essential use, then we cannot characterise or indeed make sense of the idea of an extended use.

EXAMPLE: "THEIR GREEN SHOPS"

The following extract from Milton's *Comus* is commented upon by F. R. Leavis in *Revaluation*. His comments are reproduced along with the extract as an example of reference to associations in the analysis of poetry.

> Wherefore did Nature powre her bounties forth,
> With such a full and unwithdrawing hand,
> Covering the earth with odours, fruits, and flocks,
> Thronging the Seas with spawn innumerable,
> But all to please, and sate the curious taste?
> And set to work millions of spinning Worms,
> That in their green shops weave the smooth-hair'd silk
> To deck her Sons, and that no corner might
> Be vacant of her plenty, in her own loyns
> She hutch'd th'all—worshipt ore, and precious gems
> To store her children with;
>
> Milton, Comus

And set to work millions of spinning Worms,
That in their green shops weave the smooth-hair'd silk . . .

The Shakespearean life of this is to be explained largely by the swift diversity of associations that are run together. The impression of the swarming worms is telescoped with that of the ordered industry of the workshop and a further vividness results from the contrasting 'green', with its suggestion of leafy tranquillity. 'Smooth-hair'd' plays off against the energy of the verse the tactual luxury of stroking human hair or the living coat of an animal.

F. R. Leavis, *Revaluation*

Should one call "their green shops" a metaphor, and if so, does it exemplify an extended use of the word "shop"? One might well say that to call leafy branches green shops implies an extended use of the word "shop", but on what grounds? What essential characteristic of a shop has been ignored? What is incorporated by the expression which conflicts with the essential notion of a shop? There are of course differences between things commonly called shops and *these* green shops. But there are also similarities, and there seems no way of determining in the abstract which are more important, the differences or the similarities. The point may be brought out forcibly by considering tables or chairs. A Victorian chair or table is enormously different from a medieval chair or table, and both differ from modern examples. But these differences, striking though they are, do not lead us to say that calling a modern chair a chair is using the word "chair" metaphorically. Moreover, we cannot justify this unwillingness by pointing to essential similarities between Victorian, modern and medieval chairs, for they have nothing in common apart from being chairs except their use to sit on, and this cannot be the essence of being a chair since many things used to sit on are not chairs.

A similar procedure may be adopted for the word "shop",

for a shop may be, but need not be, a building; it may be, but need not be, a place where things are sold; and it may be, but need not be, a place where things are made. We want to say that, for many words: (1) there is a normal use of the word 'x'; (2) there are essential characteristics of the things usually called xs; (3) there are extended uses of the word 'x'; and (4) in these cases some of the essential characteristics are missing. However, since we cannot usually maintain (1) and (2) by saying what the essential characteristics in question are (there normally are none), we cannot justify either (3) or (4).

One cannot say that the metaphorical use of 'x' is its application to objects which *are not* commonly called xs, for this would make the normal development of language (for example, the use of "table" of new types of tables, draughtsmen's tables, or invalid tables) metaphorical, and it surely is not. Instead it might be suggested that metaphors are words given an unusual application in a context in which it seems unlikely such usage will become common. (In fact metaphorical usage commonly becomes standard usage— but by then, of course, this development is no longer unlikely.)

Suppose that I have just invented what will in fact be called a draughtsman's table and that the question is whether to call it a table or a desk. Since the issue is posed in these terms viz., Is it a table or a desk?—hence, presumably, we understand both "It's a table" and "It's a desk" when they are applied to this new object—it seems that no one would have any reason to feel puzzled about what I meant if I chose to call it a table. Further, my decision, if it received general acceptance would resolve a difficulty of classification. But there is no such problem of classification to which a man might contribute as a solution the judgement that his mistress is a (or the) sun. It is unlikely that we have felt any need to apply one of the terms, "sun", "moon", "planet" or "star", to this or any other person or that we would have posed the question in the form, "Is she a sun, or moon etc?" Consequently if someone were to remark "She is a sun", instead of solving a problem he would create one. What does he mean? What can he think might be conveyed by the remark?

We had reasons for calling the draughtsman's table a table and counter reasons for calling it a desk. Neither set was logically compelling—neither reflected necessary or sufficient conditions for the use of the words "table" and "desk". But though they were opposed both carried some weight, both were felt to be good so that a decision one way or the other was required. But if a man said "My Mistress is a sun", our minds would not be focused upon particular similarities and differences—we would not already feel pressed to a decision by an awareness of good reasons both for calling her a sun and for calling her a moon. One reason for this difference between the cases might be that while it appears plain that a draughtsman's table is a piece of furniture, hence that it is either a table or a desk or a chair etc., there seems no comparably unproblematic description of a woman which might force us to classify her as sun, moon or planet. The unproblematic description 'body' divides immediately into 'heavenly' and 'earthly'—woman falling naturally into the second category. But whatever the reason the result of the difference is that were someone to remark "My Mistress is a sun", we should not know what considerations had been at issue—what similarities were, in the making of the remark, judged important, what differences ignored. We should have to imagine what reasons might be advanced for addressing a woman in this way and then decide which of these the speaker had in mind.

In fact the same kind of issue viz., In what respect is something x like an a and in what respects like a b, arises in both cases; the difference lies in the context. In the case of the table the context is one of classification, we know why we would say a and why b, the question is *which* shall we say? In the other something has already been said, the question is *why*? Nor does the fact that we have to work out what a speaker has in mind when he speaks metaphorically imply that words used metaphorically have a special kind of meaning. If someone calls a friend of mine nationalistic I may have to think before I see why this description was judged appropriate; but this does not make the description metaphorical.

From the point of view of the theory of meaning, then, no clear distinction can be drawn between metaphorical and non-metaphorical uses of words. From this it might be concluded that one should say of all language that it is metaphorical. To do so would be a mistake, for such a conclusion would deprive the word "metaphorical" of a specific sense, hence deprive *that* conclusion of any content.

CHAPTER 14

MEANING AND WHAT IS MEANT

IN the course of any discussion about meaning, either in the abstract, or in connection with the interpretation of poetry, the suggestion is inevitably made that words may, and probably do, have different meanings for different people. There seem to be three ways in which one may come to form, or seek to defend, such an opinion.

The first way is by argument from the possibility that our sensory experiences differ to the conclusion that there may be differences in the meanings attached to some words by different people. If we suppose that one person's colour experiences may differ from another's so that the world may look very different to different people, or if we suppose that different people may experience pleasure and pain differently, then, so it is argued, the words for colours and for pleasures and pains may well have different meanings for different people, even though they may appear to use them in the same way.

A second way is to draw attention to such events as the following:

- A man stops in conversation and turns pale at the words "Pearl Harbor".
- A woman shrieks hysterically when she hears the words "Ravensbruck" or "Auschwitz".
- A poet in a love poem speaks of "cigarette-paper leaves".
- A novelist sets all his events against a background of velvet lawns and spreading oaks.

The following comments then seem to be appropriate:

– Pearl Harbor has a special meaning for him.

– Auschwitz has a special meaning for her.

– Cigarette paper has a particular meaning for the poet.

– Velvet lawns etc. mean something special to the novelist.

Moreover it might seem natural in the last two cases to go further in suggesting what the special meaning might be, and how perceiving it could contribute to the understanding of the poem or novel.

Finally, a third way derives from noticing examples like these. A poet portrays a worm as destroying a rose, yet the poem does not appear to be dealing with horticulture. In several poems, he apparently interrupts the flow of thought with lines about a rainbow. In another he describes a desert in such a way as to make it seem peculiarly significant. About these cases we might be inclined to make the following comments:

– For him the worm means, or stands for, corrupting morality or evil.

– For him the rainbow means, or stands for, joy or peace.

– For him the desert means, or stands for, life on earth.

Once again, one would perhaps be inclined to interpret the poems in the light of these comments.

Each of these three lines of thought must be examined more closely.

THE FIRST CASE: DIFFERENCES IN EXPERIENCE

One would expect it to be true that where experiences are different, uses of words will be different. A person who is colour-blind, or who never experiences physical pleasure, will reveal this by inadequacies in his use of colour-words, or words describing pleasure. But we are to envisage a case in which differences in experience do not result in an inadequate use of words. Two people, it is claimed, might both use colour-words perfectly well, making the same discriminations, calling the same things red, green, yellow and so on, and yet they might perceive coloured things quite differently. They might both see the same *number* of colours but the things that *A* sees as green might look to *B* as the things *A* sees as red look to *A*, and so also for blue and orange, and purple and yellow. We are to suppose that *A* and *B* make the same discriminations between colours, and describe the same objects by· the same colour-words, but that the colour experience which *A* associates with the word "red" is quite different from the one *B* associates with "red". It is argued that in such circumstances we should say that what *A* means by "red" is different from what *B* means by it.

Let us examine the argument in more detail. It requires us to do three things:

(1) to suppose that we all use words in the same way;

(2) to imagine that our experencies may differ in ways described;

(3) to conclude, as a result, that colour-words may *mean* different things to different people although they *use* them in the same way. But in fact we cannot do both of the first two things without inconsistency. It follows that there is no reason for doing the third.

The reason why it is impossible to imagine both that people use colour-words in the same way and that their colour experiences differ is that such a situation *cannot be described*. The fact that we all use colour-words in the same way makes it impossible to describe (or imagine) differences in our colour experiences. An attempt to do so might take the following course:

– *A*: When you and I look at a thing we both call red, for

example, a pillar box, maybe it really looks different to each of us. Perhaps it looks red to you but green to me.

– *B*: But if pillar-box looks green to you, you are colour-blind, for it must look like grass to you and this shows that you do not discriminate between the colour of grass and the colour of pillar-boxes.

– *A*: No. I am not suggesting that the pillar-box looks like grass to me, only that it looks green (and correspondingly that grass looks red).

– *B*: But to say that something looks green is just to say that it looks like grass; what else could it mean? If you say the pillar-box looks green to you and deny that it looks like grass I do not know what you mean by green; you might as well say it looks jubbly.

– *A*: I mean it looks to me the way grass looks to you.

– *B*: But what way is that if it is not green?

A cannot express the thought he has, the situation he wants to imagine. What he says will always either show him to be colour-blind, or commit him to nonsense. The reason for this is quite simple. *A* cannot succeed in his attempt because it is inconsistent with assumptions we have made about him, in particular that neither he nor *B* is colour-blind, that they do both use words in the same way. To say that two people use "green" in the same way is to say at least that they call the same things "green". It follows that if one says grass is green then the other does too. And if one says that something looks green, he must mean that it looks like green things, i.e. things everyone agrees to be green, for example, grass. *A* wished to say that the pillar-box looked green while denying that it looked like green things (e.g. grass). But in saying one and denying the other he contradicts himself. In fact *A* can only explain what the pillar-box looks like to him by comparing the way it looks with the way other things look. But if he compares it with other red things he tells us nothing surprising, while if he compares it with green things he shows himself to be colour-blind.

The first way of arguing that words may mean different things to different people, then, is no way at all. It seems as though it ought to be a possibility, but it is not. However, even if it were possible to imagine these differences in experience, it would not follow that colour words had different meanings for different people. As was argued in Chapter 13, the meaning of what we say is not to be discovered by asking what images we have in our minds when we say it.

THE SECOND CASE: AUSCHWITZ

Clearly people with different past lives and experiences react differently. A man who has been through a concentration camp may well react emotionally on hearing the name of the camp. One whose sex-life has in some bizarre way involved cigarette-papers may remember rather unusual things when he sees cigarette-papers or hears the word. In general the things we think of, remember and feel when something is seen or mentioned, differ considerably. For this reason one may quite properly say that Auschwitz means something special to this person, cigarette-paper to that, and so on. This does not, however, imply that these people would use the words to refer to different things, that the words would have different meanings for them in this *linguistic* sense. They would agree that "Pearl Harbor" means a place in the Pacific, "Auschwitz" means a place in Europe, "cigarette-paper" means paper used in rolling cigarettes, and "velvet lawns, etc." means grass of a certain kind, etc. In other words, one is not denying that the words call to mind in these people just the same places and things that they do in us. The difference between us is that the events, places and things *themselves* are especially important in these people's lives. It is not the *words* which have a special meaning, it is the things and places, and they have a special meaning in the sense simply that they are vividly remembered, or that the thought of them arouses strong emotions. To say that cigarette-paper has a special meaning for Millabell does not imply that if I ask him for a cigarette-paper he will misunderstand me, or that he will use the term in an aberrant way. I could not discover this special meaning by investigating Millabell's use of the term. Rather I should have to investigate his past life and practices. It follows that, although discoveries about a person's past life may help us to see which *things* have a special meaning for him, such discoveries will not enable us to say that he means something special by the *word* he uses to refer to those things.

THE THIRD CASE: SYMBOLISM

Writers do often use words to convey something more or other than they normally convey. This happens, too, in ordinary life; the language of sexual comment and suggestion is full of indirect reference and symbolism. There are, however, some striking differences between this type of 'special' meaning and the last.

(1) When words are used to convey something other than what they normally convey, or something is referred to as a symbol, there is frequently a convention which applies. It is a poetic convention that a rose is a symbol of

love. It is a convention (one amongst others) of ordinary speech that "the bathroom" is used to refer to the lavatory. Moreover, a man may set up conventions of his own over a period of time, either in his speech, or in his writing.

(2) But metaphors and symbols do not work because the objects in question have a special meaning for the writer or reader in the sense earlier discussed. They work because the reader or hearer can see what the author is trying to convey by them, and because he can see how they might express what the writer or speaker wishes to convey. If I tell some-one that I have pain which sometimes boils and sometimes simmers, it will be immediately clear to him what the difference is. But this does not depend on, nor is it related to, any special concern on my part or on his with boiling and simmering. They may mean nothing to either of us, yet what I mean by what I say will be clear.

(3) Auschwitz and cigarette-paper may each mean some-thing special to someone, but it would be absurd to suggest translating them, or to suggest that the words "Auschwitz" and "cigarette-paper" require translation when uttered by these people. With metaphors and symbolic references translation may be difficult (in many cases it is easy), but it is never inappropriate or absurd. Besides, it makes sense to speak of getting the meaning of a metaphor or symbol right, or getting it wrong. By contrast there would be no sense in saying that one had got the meaning of "cigarette-paper" wrong if one failed to see that cigarette-paper had a special meaning for someone.

Metaphors have meaning in just the same way that ordinary words have meaning, even though there is some-thing unordinary about them. Ordinary language contains an enormous element of metaphor or near-metaphor.

Indeed, as was argued in the last chapter it is impossible in general to distinguish its metaphorical from its non-metaphorical use. A metaphor only has meaning because it functions as a part, albeit a somewhat unusual part of language. When, therefore, we say that the word "desert" is used metaphorically in a poem, and that the poet gives it a special meaning, we mean no more than that he uses the word to refer to, or characterise, things which the word does not in common usage refer to or characterise.

MEANING AND INTENTION

There are times when we do not know quite what to make of a passage of prose, an event in a novel, a poem or a picture. When in doubt we tend to resort to one of two methods of finding an answer. We may say that what it means depends on our reactions to it (we saw the weaknesses in this line in discussing the causal theory). On the other hand, we may say that what it means can only be discovered by finding out what the writer or painter intended it to mean. This raises the general question of the relationship between an artist's or writer's intentions and the meaning of his work.

There must be limits upon the amount of attention we pay to the intentions of a writer or artist. Suppose that someone wrote "Fred fried an egg for Mary" and later said that he intended this to mean "Fred worshipped Mary from afar". We should have to say that, whatever the writer intended, the first sentence could not mean the second. Similarly, if a poet were to write "He set his flute to her white-bellied lute" and in his diary say that he meant by this line "How careless of consequence is the modern youth". We should again have to say that the first could not mean the second (though there are other interpretations which we could accept). Of course in both cases we assume the writers are not writing in code. But unless they are using a code it is impossible to pay any attention to their statements of intention since one cannot otherwise see how their words can be taken in the way they suggest. If we do not believe that something q can be conveyed by a sentence p, then we cannot say that p means or meant q.

A person does not have complete liberty to interpret his own utterances by saying that he intended this or that by them. There are innumerable situations in which one might say that so-and-so could not have intended such-and-such by such-and-such. In general one can only say of a man that he intended something y by an action x if it is possible to do y by doing x, or, if it is not possible, if he is ignorant of its impossiblity. When interpreting language we can only say of a man that he intended q by p (where p and q are sentences) if it is possible to convey q by p, or given that it is not, if he fails to recognise this. If, then, it is impossible to convey something q by a sentence p, we can only suppose that a writer or speaker intended to convey q by p if we also suppose him ignorant of the language and of its use. Since on the whole this is not an appropriate criticism of writers, we tend not to attribute such intentions to them. In other words, far from using a man's expressed intentions to discover what he meant, we generally determine what a man could have intended by examining what he said or wrote, by looking at his utterances or writings themselves.

Normally we do not have a writer's or artist's statement about what he intended to convey in a particular poem or painting, so that our problem is to make out his intention from the work itself. But, even if we did have a statement, we would still have to use the poem or painting as a touch-stone in terms of which to judge how seriously to take it. It is a general truth that people make mistakes about what they intend and, perhaps more important, fail to execute intentions, sometimes unknowingly. For example a person might say, when asked what his intention was in doing something, that he was fertilising the roses when in fact he was poisoning them. A man might intend to placate some-one but succeed only in infuriating him. These are cases of failure to fulfil an intention. Sometimes in such cases one realises that one has failed, at other times, for example, in intending to convince someone of one's sincerity, one may think one has succeeded and be wrong.

Indeed a writer or artist may himself attempt to work out from his poem or painting what he intended by it. Just as we puzzle over a picture or poem and wonder what it means, so the artist or author may himself look at his work and ask himself what he meant by it, what he intended when he made it. If he now states what his intention was his statement has no more authority than anyone else's; he, like us, looks at the poem or painting and tries to see what could have been intended.

Although the words and sentences a man uses limit the possible interpretations of his work, hence what he can be said to have meant by it, they may still leave open a variety of interpretative questions. What a man says, or means, is not solely determined by the words and sentences he utters. Whether, for example, if I say "He is insane", I mean that Jones is insane, or that Brown is, will depend on which of them I intend to refer to. The question what is meant, where there is ambiguity of reference, concerns the intentions of a writer or speaker. The same is true where the meaning of a passage depends on whether or not it contains an allusion. Words and sentences cannot refer or allude; these are activities of speakers and writers. Consequently to say that a passage contains a particular reference or allusion (given that it is not explicit) is to say that the writer intended to make that reference or allusion. Cioffi is surely right in claiming (in his paper, 'Intention and Interpretation in Criticism', *PAS* LXIV (1963–4)) that we could not take Yeats's lines,

> What young mother a shape upon her lap
> Honey of generation had betrayed,
> (from Among School Children)

as alluding to Porphyry's essay, or consequently interpret them by reference to it, if we knew that Yeats was ignorant of the essay.

Whether a poem is ironical too is a matter of intention, for, once again, words and sentences do not express attitudes, people do.

However, where a word or sentence is ambiguous, or where symbolism allows various interpretations, the choice of one reading in preference to another is not determined by knowledge of the writer's intentions. What a man *meant* is of course a matter of his intentions when he wrote, but a phrase or a passage may *have* a meaning which the writer never envisaged. Cioffi takes an example from Hopkins's poem *Henry Purcell* where the phrase "fair fall" can be taken in two ways, though Hopkins claims to have been unaware of this when he wrote it. Cioffi argues that we must take the phrase in the way Hopkins intended. If we reject what he *says* he meant by it in favour of an alternative reading it can only be because we believe he *really* intended it to be read in this way.

Now if we feel compelled to select one of the possible meanings of an ambiguous passage as *the* meaning, it is very likely that we shall choose the one we believe to have been intended by the author. But we shall only feel this compulsion if our main interest in a work is to discover what its author meant. If our interest is in the work itself, there seems no reason why we should not regard it as having several possible meanings, as we regard a piece of music as capable of various interpretations. We might even have an interest in changes in popular fashions of interpretation. So long as we are clear that there are these different interests we shall not be tempted to pursue fruitless questions as to *the true meaning* of ambiguous passages.

CHAPTER 15

A THEORY OF MEANING

WHAT can be said about meaningfulness? Can we say what it is for a word to have a meaning? These questions raise one of the most difficult of philosophical problems. As we have seen, the problem is not to find something which, by its relationship to the word, gives it a meaning, an effect on a hearer, an object or a set of objects which a word pictures or stands for, a definition or an essence. A word has a meaning only in the sense that it has a use and a word's use is clearly not a further thing. It is a characteristic of utterances of the word itself—of the manner of its employment.

Many things have uses but not everything which has a use is said to have a meaning. Our problem, then, is to discover what is distinctive about words. There seem to be several possible approaches to it. One might examine the way the use of 'x' is taught or transmitted, or the kinds of things 'x' is used to do, or the *way* in which 'x' is used to do what it is used to do. Let us adopt the first approach.

A man learns to use a fishing rod or a hammer by practising various movements with these instruments. When he can perform these movements he has learnt the use of these instruments. To teach a man to use a rod is to teach him to make the same or similar movements in the same pattern as oneself. What do we teach a man to do in the same way as ourselves when we teach him to use a word (and I am thinking now only of common nouns, verbs and adjectives)? The answer seems to be that we teach him to use it of, or in the presence of, the same kinds of thing, or in the same kinds of situations as we do.

It might seem that the proper test of whether a pupil uses a word in the same situations as his teacher is that he uses it of the appropriate objects, "dog" of dogs, "cat" of cats and "table" of tables, etc., etc. But this suggestion will not do, for suppose that I introduce a new word "jibbidy-wock" and suppose that I get someone to judge correctly when I am going to use it. Clearly I have taught him to use it in the same way and in the same situations as I do. But have I taught him to use it of jibbidywocks? The only test of whether or not there is a jibbidywock about when he uses the word is my say-so, since I invented the word and taught him how to use it. The question, then, whether a pupil uses a word 'x' of xs i.e. whether he uses it in the same *situations* as his teacher is really the same as the question whether he uses it on the same *occasions* as his teacher. The situations in which a teacher, teaching a pupil to use 'x', uses 'x' are, ipso facto, x situations. The test, then, of whether the pupil uses a word in the same kinds of situations as his teacher is that he uses it when and only when the teacher uses it. However in order to exclude the possibility that the pupil might be parroting the teacher's utterances, we must stipulate that he use the word in *anticipation* of the teacher's use of it, as we do when a child is learning the multiplication tables. We asked earlier what a teacher of language gets his pupil to do in the same way as he does. The answer is that he teaches him when to utter the word, i.e. to anticipate the occasions on which he will use it.

We are now able to define the conditions under which two words 'x' and 'y' have different meanings or uses as those in which a pupil being taught and learning to use both 'x' and 'y' is given different tuition for the two words, for example, sometimes when the pupil guesses the teacher will use both 'x' and 'y' only one is correct (the teacher only uses one). The definition of identity of use is more complicated, but we can say that a pupil has been taught the same use for two words if the tuition in both cases has been identical. Notice that, on this theory, although we can say that two words have the same use, there is no other way of saying what a word's use is.

The account so far of what it is for something to have a use in the way words do is too wide. As it stands it fits the case of a farmer teaching a farmhand how to apply fertiliser or how to use fertiliser, for knowing how to use fertiliser, is, also, knowing when to use it. Yet we would hardly call learning to apply fertiliser learning the use of a word, or say that the use of fertiliser is like the use of a word, or that, having a use, it therefore has a meaning. Let us assume nevertheless that the account is, though too wide, substantially correct, i.e. that to say that a word has a meaning is to say that its use can be taught in the way described. But let us look for further characteristics of words which distinguish them from such things as fertiliser. There are three striking differences.

(1) Having been taught to recognise the conditions of soil, weather and plant growth in which fertiliser is to be applied a farmer does not go on to use fertiliser to communicate; he uses it to influence the growth of crops. Words on the other hand are not used to bring about changes in the world except indirectly through communication with someone. So there is a difference in the uses to which the farmer puts his fertilising skill and the pupil his verbal skill after they have been acquired.

(2) Because a fertiliser is used to change crop growth there

are two ways of asking whether the farmhand has correctly applied the fertiliser. One may ask first: Does he apply it as he was taught? Here the method used by the farmer who taught him is the standard of correctness; the correct way is the way in which *he* does it. But one may also ask: Does the farmhand's way of applying it actually improve the crops, or is there a better way? The latter question seems at first sight out of place in relation to words, there seems to be no analogous question in this case.

(3) If teaching someone to apply fertiliser in certain conditions of weather, soil, crop-size, etc. were exactly like teaching the use of a word, then unless it were an exceptional 'word' (one having synonyms), there would be no way of indicating or describing the conditions in which to apply it except by actually applying fertiliser. If we teach someone to use the word "red", he cannot say to what property of things he correctly applies the word "red" except by using "red". Suppose now that in order to teach someone the use of a 'word' for red we teach him not to utter "red" but to apply a certain type of paint to the thing in question with a brush. In these circumstances he will be unable to describe the property of things to which he applies the paint with a brush except by applying the paint to them with a brush. It is, then, a peculiarity of language and perhaps its distinguishing mark that any account of the conditions under it is correct to use a given word usually involves the use of that word. This may also be true of the teaching of some skills involving complex judgements about conditions (perhaps even the application of fertilisers), but it does not seem to be *necessarily* true of them.

Three striking differences emerge, then, between words and something like fertiliser, despite the similarity in the way their use can be conveyed.

Perhaps the most striking is the first. We call words those things which, when we have learnt to use them, we use to communicate. What is it to use something to communicate? It is important to notice that the farmhand *might* use the application of fertiliser to communicate information. But he could do so only under certain complex conditions, conditions which would make his application of fertiliser a conventional rather than an agricultural performance. He might set out to apply fertiliser intending thereby to direct his neighbour's attention to the condition of the crops. He might even seek to deceive his neighbour as to the condition of soil, weather and crops by applying fertiliser when it was not fertiliser-time. But in neither case is he really communicating; he is merely causing someone to think something, as one might get another to think that one is dead by pretending to be dead. (Remember the case of the Yeti tracks in Chapter 10.) However, if we suppose that the neighbour formed certain beliefs about the condition of soil, weather and crops not just because the farmhand was spreading fertiliser, but because he recognised that the farmhand intended to induce these beliefs in him by his fertiliser-spreading, and if we further suppose that the farmhand intended him to recognise that he intended this, we begin to approach a communication situation. Complicated conditions about intentions such as these are used by H. P. Grice ('Meaning', *Philosophical Review* 66 (1957)) in an attempt to distinguish cases in which *A gets B* to believe something by doing something from cases in which *A tells B* something by doing something, i.e. communicates. Only in the latter case, he argues, can one speak of meaning in the linguistic sense. In fact the full account of communication, as given by Grice and extended by P. F. Strawson ('Intention and Convention in Speech Acts', *Philosophical Review* 73 (1964)) is considerably more complicated than the example above suggests. It involves a whole hierarchy of recognitions of intentions.

According to Grice, then, what distinguishes words is not the way in which their use is taught, or the kind of skill we impart when we teach their different uses. Things which are not words may be similar to them in these respects. He takes things (Yeti tracks, fertiliser spreading), which have a tendency to induce beliefs, and asks in what circumstances we would call using them to induce such beliefs, communicating. His answer is that they must be used in the context of certain intentions and recognitions of intention. Grice concludes that a thing has linguistic meaning if it is used to induce a belief in this kind of context.

Speech, however, consists of utterances of sounds which have on the whole no tendency to induce beliefs in anyone not trained in their use. Moreover, training someone to use them in the way described earlier in this chapter does not convert them into things, like Yeti tracks, which induce beliefs simply by their occurrence (i.e. they are not converted into natural signs). Consequently the issue, in deciding whether such a sound is a word or has a meaning, can not be whether or not the intention is to exploit, in a non-communicating way, the sound's power to induce beliefs—it has no such power.

One cannot suppose people to intend the impossible and it would be absurd to intend to convey a belief by uttering a sound when no one had been trained in its use. On the other hand, once such training has occurred the suggestion that the sound is being used as a natural sign, i.e. to induce beliefs by exploiting its causal connections with other things, is equally absurd. It seems, then, that although words are distinctively used to communicate they cannot be defined by reference to intentions involved in communicating. We cannot, then, regard its use in communication as a necessary condition of something being a word, hence we cannot refuse to call learning to spread fertiliser, learning to use a word, simply because the skill is not likely to be employed in communicating.

A further clue to the distinction between those things, using which is using a part of language, and those things, like fertiliser-spreading, using which is not, lies in the second distinctive characteristic of words mentioned above. The striking thing about fertiliser is that it is used to change things, and that tuition in its use consists in training people to use it when it will produce certain effects. Consequently although one may be trained to use it in specific conditions of soil, weather and crops, it use will nevertheless be correct whenever it produces the right results. Although a word may be used to produce effects, tuition in its use does not, and could not, consist in training someone to use it when it produces such effects. Words can be used to produce effects only because people have been tutored in their use. Fertiliser-spreading produces effects whether anyone has been trained to use it or not. A word's use is endowed on it by, and only by, someone teaching someone else to use it.

If, now, we add the third characteristic of words mentioned earlier it is possible to define linguistic meaning. To say that something has a meaning, or is a word, is to say that it has a use (i.e. someone can teach another to use it) and that the transmission of the skill of using it consists in teaching someone when to use it and when not. Two further conditions are, however, required. First, the possibility of someone using it to produce any effect upon another (except one explicable solely by its physical properties) depends on both having learned how to use it. Second, the conditions under which it is correct to use it cannot in general be described without its use. The use of all words cannot be acquired by verbal instruction or from a dictionary.

We use words for a variety of purposes, most of which are not marked by specific linguistic items or forms, e.g. the use of "bring" in ordering soup as distinct from its use in ordering fish. Three purposes which *are* marked in this way are the use of a word to say that something is the case, to tell someone to do something, and to ask a question. Corresponding to these purposes are the grammatical distinctions between indicative, imperative and interrogative sentences.

Marks which distinguish these three types of utterance are clearly meaningful; using them wrongly may result in a meaningless utterance. Equally the function they have is quite different from that of common nouns, adjectives and verbs. The question arises whether the sense in which these marks have meaning is covered by the present theory. The theory is that a word has a meaning if its use can be taught, and the criterion of success in teaching is a certain change in the relationship between the utterances of pupil and teacher. Now, *that* account of teaching the use of a word made the utterances of both teacher and pupil appear very like indicative utterances. It is easy to imagine, however, two rather different teaching situations in relation to either of which we could formulate a criterion of successful teaching but in which the utterances of teacher or pupil might seem more like imperative or interrogative utterances. In the former case the test of the pupil's skill might be the degree of coincidence between the teacher's utterances before and after some action by the pupil. In the latter, it might be the degree of coincidence between a pupil's utterance and a subsequent utterance by the teacher—the teacher's antecedent utterances being disregarded. Further one could also imagine the roles being changed about, the pupil sometimes seeming to ask the questions or issue the orders.

If these three teaching situations were marked by some variation in the form of utterances and if a pupil learned to use words in all of them, then, clearly, he would have learnt the use of these marks also. In other words a pupil's success in learning to use words in several sorts of situation will serve as a criterion of his ability to use and recognise marks of grammatical mood. It seems, then, that the theory is well able to deal with 'grammatical meaning'.

The present theory was devised partly to meet the inadequacies of other theories, but also, in part, to support a view of mental concepts. Like other theories of meaning it has a metaphysical purpose. According to the theory there is no reason to suppose that because one can teach the meaning of a word one can point to something else in virtue of which one applies it. Thus one can hold the view that certain statements about mental states (e.g. anger or belief) are statements about behaviour, without being required to be capable of saying in other words what this behaviour is. On the other hand, one can also affirm that other statements about mental states (e.g. pains or visual images) are not statements about behaviour, even though one cannot justify this claim by publicly displaying pains or visual images.

In making the successful teaching of its use the test of whether a word has a meaning and by denying that there is any other test (e.g. that one be able to explain why one uses it, or point out to others the things one applies it to) the theory is extremely liberal. It is common to find theories of meaning designed to restrict meaningfulness to certain sorts of words (e.g. those referring to what can be perceived by the senses) or at least to force us to interpret the meaning of all words in restricted ways. The present theory is not restricting in this way. But if it is to explain the undoubtedly important differences between words like "red", "table" and "hot" on the one hand and a variety of words such as "God", "soul", "good" and "ought" on the other, the theory will require considerable elaboration. Such elaboration might for example take the form of investigations into the different circumstances in which, and procedures by which, different words are learned. Thus it might be discovered that whereas learning to use "God" involved learning a ritual, or perhaps adopting a certain code of behaviour, it required no skill in sorting or identifying Gods. By contrast learning to use "red" or "chair" might be mainly the acquisition of skill in sorting and identifying colours and furniture. Again learning to use "Hello" would seem to be almost entirely a matter of learning a ritual. Words learned in such different circumstances are likely to be used for quite different purposes. One would expect the assessment of utterances in which they occur to be correspondingly different.

To speak of meaning as an image or a definition or an object, something one can as it were lay one's hands on, suggests that getting to know the meaning of a word is like a single act of acquaintance or comprehension. One of the interests in the theory of meaning as use is that it directs attention to the variety of activities and circumstances in which we must learn to use a word if we are to be said to understand its meaning, or know its use. I shall give two examples.

Consider first the word "coin". Winch, in *The Idea of Social Science*, argues that one cannot tell simply by observation what a man is doing. If we observed someone giving another a coin we should (simply from this observation) describe him, inadequately, as handing over a piece of metal. But of course Winch's point really concerns the meaning of "coin". To understand what "coin" means, to learn its meaning, we need to observe its use in a complex variety of contexts. We may also need to observe the use of other related words such as "value" and "exchange". In effect we must know something about the institution of money. Now to decide whether something is a coin requires comparably complex observation for we only call something a coin if it plays a certain role in social life. Consequently we need to observe a great deal more than one transaction to know that the object involved was a coin or that the action was a payment.

Even colour words present complexities. In determining whether a man uses them correctly, i.e. knows their meaning, we must examine not only his ability to discriminate but the circumstances in which or the means by which he discriminates. Doubt would be thrown on a man's understanding of colour words if it were discovered that he could use them correctly only with the aid of a light-frequency meter or if, though normally he used them correctly, he failed to distinguish the figures on the Ishahara test cards.

Apart from the metaphysical issues which hinge on questions of meaning, and apart from the intrinsic interest of the subject there is another interest to be derived from discussing theories of meaning. Disputes about and investigations into the meaning of a word, or line, or passage will be conducted in different ways depending on what the question "what does this mean?" is taken to mean e.g. What is the definition? What associations does this bring to mind? What is the implication of the events recorded? What did the author intend? To what did the author allude or refer? Each question calls for a different kind of research; the first calls for a study of the dictionary, the second, and probably the third too, for a psychological survey, the fourth for a complex investigation of literary conventions, the writer's preoccupations and perhaps his eccentricities of expression, the fifth for biographical research. But none of these researches taps that essential to the whole enterprise, our knowledge of our own tongue. A central purpose of the second part of this book has been to separate out these different questions about meaning and to set them apart from another sense of the question "what is the meaning of this word or sentence?" that sense in which merely to speak the language to which the word or sentence belongs is to know the answer.

FURTHER READING

CHAPTERS 1–4

General

Braithwaite, R. B. *Scientific Explanation*. Cambridge University Press, 1953.

Feigl, H., and Brodbeck, M. (ed.). *Readings in the Philosophy of Science*. Appleton-Century-Crafts, 1953.

Hempel, C. G. *Aspects of Scientific Explanations and Other Essays*. The Free Press, Glencoe, 1965.

—— *The Philosophy of Natural Science*. Prentice-Hall, 1966.

Kneale, W. *Probability and Induction*. The Clarendon Press, 1949.

Nagel, E. *The Structure of Science*. Harcourt, Brace and World, 1961.

Passmore, J. 'Explanation in Everyday Life, in Science, and in History', *History and Theory*, II. Wesleyan University Press, Middletown, Connecticut, 1962.

Explanation Prediction and Deduction

Hospers, J. 'What is Explanation', in A. N. Flew (ed.), *Essays in Conceptual Analysis*, II. Macmillan, 1956.

Hempel, C. G. 'The Logic of Explanation', in H. Feigl and M. Brodbeck (ed.), *Readings in the Philosophy of Science*.

Popper, K. R. *The Logic of Scientific Discovery*. Hutchinson, 1959.

Scriven, M. 'Definitions Explanations and Theories', in *Minnesota Studies in The Philosophy of Science*, Vol. II, ed. H. Feigl, M. Scriven and G. Maxwell. University of Minnesota Press.

Causation and Induction

Collingwood, R. G. *An Essay in Metaphysics*. Oxford University Press, 1940.

Goodman, N. *Fact, Fiction and Forecast*. Bobbs-Merrill, 1965.

Hart, H. L. A., and Honoré, A. M. *Causation in the Law*. Oxford University Press, 1959.

Mill, J. S. *A System of Logic*, Bk. III. Longmans, Green, 1906.

Russell, B. 'On the Notion of Cause', in *Mysticism and Logic*. Longmans, Green, 1921.

—— *The Problems of Philosophy*. Home University Library, 1964.

Von Wright, G. F. *The Logical Problem of Induction*. Oxford University Press, 1957.

CHAPTER 5

Marx, M. (ed.). *Theories in Contemporary Psychology*. Macmillan, 1965.

—— and Hillix, W. A. *Systems and Theories in Psychology*. McGraw-Hill, 1963.

Minnesota Studies in the Philosophy of Science, Vol. I. University of Minnesota Press, 1963.

Ryle, G. *The Concept of Mind*. Penguin, 1963.

Skinner, B. F. *Science and Human Behaviour*. Macmillan, 1964.

White, A. *Explaining Human Behaviour*. Hull University Press, 1962.

CHAPTER 6

Collingwood, R. G. *The Idea of History*. Oxford University Press, 1961.

Evans-Pritchard, E. E. *Nuer Religion*. Oxford University Press, 1956.

Hempel, C. G. 'The Logic of Functional Analysis', in *Symposium on Sociological Theory*, ed. Llewllyn Gross. Row, Peterson and Co., 1959.

Homans, G. 'Contemporary Theory in Sociology', in R. E. L. Faris (ed.). *Handbook of Sociology*. Rand, McNally, Chicago, 1966.

Nagel, E. 'The Formalization of Functionalism', in *Logic Without Metaphysics and Other Essays in the Philosophy of Science*. The Free Press, Glencoe, 1956.

White, A. (ed.). *The Philosophy of Action*. Oxford University Press, 1968.

Winch, P. *The Idea of Social Science*. Routledge and Kegan Paul, 1958.

CHAPTER 7

Collingwood, R. G. *The Idea of History*.

Danto, A. C. *Analytical Philosophy of History*. Cambridge University Press, 1965.

Dray, W. H. *Laws and Explanation in History*. Cambridge University Press, 1957.

—— *Philosophy of History*. Prentice-Hall, 1964.

Gardiner, P. (ed.). *Theories of History*. The Free Press, Glencoe, 1959.

Hempel, C. G. 'The Function of General Laws in History', in *Theories of History*, ed. P. Gardiner.

Hook, S. (ed.). *Philosophy and History*. New York University Press, 1963.

Meyerhoff, M. (ed.). *The Philosophy of History in Our Time*. Doubleday, 1959

CHAPTER 8

Beardsley, M. C. *Aesthetics*. Harcourt, Brace and World, 1958.

Edwards, P. *The Logic of Moral Discourse*. Macmillan, 1955.

Elton, W. (ed.). *The Language of Aesthetics*. Blackwell, 1959.

Sparshott, F. E. *The Structure of Aesthetics*. Toronto University Press, 1963.

Vivas, E., and Krieger, M. (ed.). *The Problems of Aesthetics*. Holt, Rinehart and Winston, 1963.

Weitz, M. *Hamlet and the Philosophy of Literary Criticism*. University of Chicago Press, 1964.

CHAPTERS 9–15

General

Alston, W. P. *Philosophy of Language*. Prentice-Hall, 1964.

Ayer, A. J. *Language, Truth and Logic.* Gollancz, 1964.

Linsky, L. (ed.). *Semantics and the Philosophy of Language.* University of Illinois Press, 1952.

Ogden, C. K., and Richards, I. A. *The Meaning of Meaning.* Routledge and Kegan Paul, 1949.

Waismann, F. *The Principles of Linguistic Philosophy*, Pt. II. Macmillan, 1968.

Wittgenstein, L. *Philosophical Investigation.* Blackwell, 1953.

CHAPTER 10

Black, M. 'The Limitations of a Behaviourist Semiotic', *Philosophical Review*, LVI. 1947.

Richards, I. A. *The Philosophy of Rhetoric.* Oxford University Press, 1936.

Russell, B. *The Analysis of Mind.* Allen and Unwin, 1961.

Stevenson, C. L. *Ethics and Language*, Ch. III. Yale University Press, 1944.

—— Black, M., and Richards, I. A. 'Symposium on Emotive Meaning', *Philosophical Review*, LVII. 1948.

CHAPTER 11

Daitz, E. 'The Picture Theory of Meaning', in *Essays in Conceptual Analysis*, ed. A. Flew. Macmillan, 1966.

Mill, J. S. *A System of Logic*, Bk. I. Longmans, Green, 1906.

Russell, B. 'On Propositions: What They are and How They Mean', in *Logic and Knowledge*, ed. R. C. Marsh, Allen and Unwin, 1956.

Ryle, G. 'The Theory of Meaning', in *British Philosophy at The mid-Century*, ed. C. A. Mace. Allen and Unwin, 1966.

CHAPTER 12

Russell, B. 'On Propositions: What They are and How They Mean'.

Ryle, G. *The Concept of Mind*, Ch. II.

Wittgenstein, L. *The Blue and Brown Books*. Blackwell, 1958.

CHAPTER 13

Alston, W. P. 'The Quest for Meanings', *Mind*, LXXII. January 1963.

Austin, J. L. 'The Meaning of a Word', in *Philosophical Papers*, ed. J. Urinson. Blackwell, 1961.

Black, M. 'Metaphor', in *Models and Metaphors*. Cornell University Press, 1961.

Quine, W. V. O. *From a Logical Point of View*, Ch. II and III. Harvard University Press, 1953.

Waismann, F. 'Verifiability' in *Logic and Language*, I, ed. A. Flew. Blackwell, 1951.

CHAPTER 14

Beardsley, M. C. *Aesthetics*.

Cioffi, F. 'Intention and Interpretation in Criticism', *Aristotelian Society Proceedings*, LXIV. 1963–4.

Sparshott, F. E. *The Structure of Aesthetics*.

Taylor, D. M. 'The Incommunicability of Content', *Mind*, LXXV. 1966.

Wimsatt, W. K., and Beardsley, M. C. 'The Intentional Fallacy', in Wimsatt, *The Verbal Icon*. University of Kentucky Press, 1954.

CHAPTER 15

Chappell, V. C. (ed.). *Ordinary Language*. Prentice-Hall, 1964.

Feyerabend, P. 'Wittgenstein's Philosophical Investigations', *Philosophical Review*, 64. 1955.

Grice, H. P. 'Meaning', *Philosophical Review*, 66. 1957.

—— 'Utterer's Meaning and Intentions', *Philosophical Review*, 78. 1969.

Strawson, P. F. 'Intention and Convention in Speech Acts', *Philosophical Review*, 73. 1964 (p. 445 and following).

INDEX